# Translation Theories Explained

*Translation Theories Explained* is a series designed to respond to the profound plurality of contemporary translation studies. There are many problems to be solved, many possible approaches that can be drawn from neighbouring disciplines, and several strong language-bound traditions plagued by the paradoxical fact that some of the key theoretical texts have yet to be translated.

Recognizing this plurality as both a strength and a potential shortcoming, the series provides a format where different approaches can be compared, their virtues assessed, and mutual blind spots overcome. There will also be scope for introductions to specific areas of translation practice. Students and scholars may thus gain comprehensive awareness of the work being done beyond local or endemic frames.

Most volumes in the series place a general approach within its historical context, giving examples to illustrate the main ideas, summarizing the most significant debates and opening perspectives for future work. The authors have been selected not only because of their command of a particular approach but also in view of their openness to alternatives and their willingness to discuss criticisms. In every respect the emphasis is on explaining the essential points as clearly and as concisely as possible, using numerous examples and providing glossaries of the main technical terms.

The series should prove particularly useful to students dealing with translation theories for the first time, to teachers seeking to stimulate critical reflection, and to scholars looking for a succinct overview of the field's present and future.

Anthony Pym
Series Editor

# Translation and Gender

*Translating in the 'Era of Feminism'*

Luise von Flotow

Routledge
Taylor & Francis Group

LONDON AND NEW YORK

First published 1997 by St Jerome Publishing and University of Ottawa Press

Published 2014 by Routledge
2 Park Square, Milton Park, Abingdon, Oxon OX14 4RN
711 Third Avenue, New York, NY 10017, USA

*Routledge is an imprint of the Taylor & Francis Group, an informa business*

Notices
Knowledge and best practice in this field are constantly changing. As new research and experience broaden our understanding, changes in research methods, professional practices, or medical treatment may become necessary.

Practitioners and researchers must always rely on their own experience and knowledge in evaluating and using any information, methods, compounds, or experiments described herein. In using such information or methods they should be mindful of their own safety and the safety of others, including parties for whom they have a professional responsibility.

To the fullest extent of the law, neither the Publisher nor the authors, contributors, or editors, assume any liability for any injury and/or damage to persons or property as a matter of products liability, negligence or otherwise, or from any use or operation of any methods, products, instructions, or ideas contained in the material herein.

ISBN 13: 978-1-900650-05-2 (pbk)

*British Library Catalguing in Publication Data*
A catalogue record for this book is available from the British Library.

*Library of Congress Cataloging in Publication Data*
A catalogue record of this book is available from the Library of Congress.

*Canadian Cataloguing in Publication Data*
Von Flotow, Luise, 1951-
    Translation and gender: translating in the 'era of feminism'
    (Perspectives on translation)
    Includes bibliographical references.
    ISBN 0-7766-0448-1
      1. Translating and interpreting. 2. Feminism and literature.
      3. Language and languages -- Sex differences. I. Title. II. Series.

Cover design by Steve Fieldhouse, Oldham, UK

# Acknowledgements

The author and publisher wish to thank the following for permission to reprint material in this volume:

The University of Chicago Press and Richard Lattimore for the Sappho poem 'Some there are who say that the fairest thing seen', translated by Richard Lattimore, in *Greek Lyrics*, 1949.

The University of Georgia Press for Louise Labé's poem 'Clère Venus', translated by Jeanne Prine, in *Women Writers of the Renaissance and Reformation*, edited by Katharina Wilson, 1988.

Princeton University Press for the Sappho poem 'He seems to me equal to the gods', translated by Anne Carson in *Eros the Bittersweet*, 1986.

# *Contents*

# Preface

This work on gender and translation has developed out of my interests in feminist explorations of gender as a cultural construct and in translation as cultural transfer. Over the past thirty years, and as a result of the women's movement, gender issues have become entangled with issues of language. Over the same period, translation studies has developed as a part of the more general turn toward cultural studies. The complexities of translational gender relations and the resulting critical work are the subject of this book.

Gender studies and translation studies are both interdisciplinary academic fields. When they are brought into relationship with one another, a number of issues intersect: cultural gender differences, the revelation and formulation of these differences in language, their transfer by means of translation into other cultural spaces where different gender conditions obtain. Questions arise about the importance of gender politics in institutions, and the gender affiliations of the translator and the critic become an issue. Language is, of course, highly pertinent to both areas of investigation; discussions of 'patriarchal language' have played an important role in feminist research on gender, and language transfer is the basic element under discussion in translation studies. Given the political weight that both feminist thinkers and the 'political correctness' reaction have assigned to language, it is clear that gender must become an issue in translation.

It is important to note that although gender studies and translation studies may be contemporaneous fields of scholarship, their development has not been parallel. Translation studies has seen rapid development in Europe over the past decade, a development doubtless fostered by a political and economic climate encouraging cultural and economic exchange between different language groups. This has also been the case in Canada, where official bilingualism has been an important catalyst triggering translation as well as academic work on translation. In the USA, translation studies still plays a somewhat minor role, though the visibility of the field has recently increased dramatically through the efforts of a number of active individuals. Gender studies has developed differently, achieving the greatest influence in North America; the 'era of feminism' that began in the late 1960s and affected academic and public life as well as 'high' and popular culture has been instrumental in shaping the historical and scholarly context of its generation. Feminist work has entered and had an impact upon almost every academic discipline. In many parts of Europe, on the other hand, there has been less academic interest in gender studies. While much academic work on gender is imported from North America (and translated), gender studies, women's studies programmes or the like – which might encourage research into specifically European situations – are rare.

My purpose is to bring these two disciplines together, making disparate information available to students of translation on both sides of the Atlantic. By describing some of the links and inter-connections between gender issues and translation studies, I hope to inform, stimulate discussion and encourage further research into the intersections of these two fields. This objective reflects a feminist activist agenda on my part, as I demonstrate to what extent gender awareness affects international discussion, research and communication. But it also reflects an academic interest in cultural studies – in the differences between cultures and the individuals within them – and the way translation both promotes and hampers understanding and interaction.

In writing this book, I have assembled diverse publications gleaned from primarily North American sources. I have also used a number of unpublished materials, most of which are of European origin. These materials were produced for the 1995 conference of the European Society for Translation Studies held in Prague, at which I organized and chaired a session on gender and translation. Since they will not be appearing in the conference proceedings, I have considered it important to cite them extensively.

My perspective has, of course, been defined by my own experience and my limitations: a North American bilingual, bicultural (immigrant) background, academic work in French, German and Québec literatures during the 'era of feminism', and literary translation. There is doubtless much material I have not been able to refer to, for instance work produced in Scandinavian countries. Still, the amount of contemporary material I did have access to has sufficed to provide an overview. The book is divided into seven chapters, starting with a historical introduction that summarizes the way the women's movement has problematized language.

In chapter 2, I examine the influences that feminist thought and writing have had on contemporary translation practice. I look at a number of 'technical' questions such as translating 'the body' and translating feminist wordplay or cultural references. The question of translators as censors of politically questionable material is also raised here, since translators in an 'era of feminism' have developed forms of resistance to texts they consider dubious. This chapter is also concerned with the translation of 'lost' women writers and the 'readability' of these authors since there exists no tradition of reading them.

Theoretical developments are the subject of chapter 3, since the practical issues discussed in chapter 2 have had an effect on more abstract concerns in translation. Gender awareness coupled with translation has brought about a revision of the normally 'invisible' role a translator plays. Taking their cue from the feminist writers they translate, translators have begun asserting their identity and justifying the subjective aspects of their work. A concomitant revision of the discourse on translational relations has led theorists to rethink metaphors such as *les belles infidèles*, which are used to describe translation in terms of gender hierarchies, and to rewrite such fundamental 'translation myths' as that of Pandora's box.

Chapter 4 presents critical work on translation. Not unlike the feminist practice of rereading, revising and supplementing canonical texts, this critical work rereads and reconsiders translations – of Simone de Beauvoir's *The Second Sex*, of Louise Labé's sonnets, of Sappho's lyric poetry. It also looks at the efforts of translators who undertake retranslations of such 'key texts' as the Bible. In discussing the reasons for re-translations and criticism – for example, glaring mistranslations or deletions – such work points to the ideological aspects of language transfer. A related element in this chapter is the recovery of 'lost' women translators and the re-evaluation of their work from the perspective of the gender-conscious 1990s.

In chapter 5 I discuss some of the criticisms addressed to work that combines gender issues with translation studies. Given the clearly partisan approach of feminist work, criticisms 'from outside feminisms' are to be expected. It is interesting that they often take the form of silence, a condition this book seeks to counteract. Criticisms 'from within feminisms' are more productive, raising issues of cultural and political differences *between* women and confronting certain 'radical' positions with pertinent questions. One type of question addresses the problem of translations that remain 'inaccessible', for instance in the case of experimental texts. Does the problem lie in the translation? How translatable is feminist writing from other societies and cultures? How meaningful is it to the translating cultures, and how can it be rendered so, if it is not? Third world writers or less-advantaged women in multi-ethnic societies have also raised questions about the 'exploitation' and misrepresentation of their texts in the name of 'first world feminisms'. What exactly is the role of the translator in making the voices of third world women heard in the West? How should she translate? For whom is she translating? Is she merely contributing to these women's exploitation, or is her work a meaningful contribution to international feminist goals?

None of these questions have been fully explored or answered. This book raises them for a readership that may be interested in further pursuing the intersections of gender and translation, a vast area of research and development in the comparatist, intercultural and supranational approaches that translation studies fosters.

Finally, chapters 6 and 7 offer some remarks on future perspectives and a concluding statement, respectively.

My work on the intersection of gender and translation was made possible by a generous post-doctoral fellowship from the Social Sciences and Humanities Research Council of Canada, which I wish to gratefully acknowledge. Without this funding I would not have been able to spend the time necessary to put this book together. I also wish to acknowledge the reading skills of Anthony Pym, series editor, whose detailed comments on the 'facts' I accumulated, my interpretations of these facts and my sometimes convoluted syntax were usually appropriate. Taking the position of a European student of translation, he queried a number of my North American assumptions. Thanks also to colleagues Sherry Simon, Jean Delisle and to series publisher Mona Baker for their support and interest; and thanks to Jane Batchelor, Karin Littau, Eithne O'Connell and Beate Thill for presenting their work at the Prague conference and making it available to me afterwards. Finally, thanks to my family of four for learning to live in relative independence.

# 1. Historical Background

When Simone de Beauvoir wrote in 1949 "on ne naît pas femme, on le devient" and when E.M. Parshley translated this in 1953 as "one is not born, but rather becomes a woman", both Beauvoir and Parshley were talking about *gender*. Though the term did not actually come into use at the time of these texts, it was undergoing rapid development twenty years later, and its users and adapters often referred back to Simone de Beauvoir's work on women's socialization.

## The Women's Movement and the Idea of Gender

In the mid to late 1960s, as post-war feminism began to develop a certain momentum along with many of the other protest movements of the time in Western Europe and North America, the notion of *gender* evolved to complement and extend that of biological sexual difference. Since biological sexual difference hardly seemed adequate to explain the differences in men's and women's societal roles and opportunities, grassroots women's movements and scholars developed and employed other tools and analytical categories in order to understand these discrepancies. Anglo-American feminist writers and theorists began to refer back to Beauvoir and explore the questions raised by her aphorism. Beauvoir suggests that a baby born with female reproductive organs does not simply grow up to be a woman. She has to turn herself into a woman, or more correctly, she *is turned* into a woman by the society she grows up in and in response to the expectations that society has of women. The final product 'woman' is a result of education and conditioning, and differs according to the dominant influences she is subject to in the culture, subculture, ethnic group, religious sect, in which she grows up. Early feminist use of the term *gender* referred to the result of the social process that turns young females into girls, and later into women. This process instills into girls and women the physical, psychological and sociocultural attributes that are typical of a particular time and culture and which, as a rule, differ substantially from the attributes of the men of the same period.

It needs to be stressed here that *gender* refers to the sociocultural construction of *both* sexes. Feminist thinkers of the late 1960s and early 1970s developed the term in the interests of examining and understanding women's socialized difference from men, and their concomitant cultural and political powerlessness. More recently, though, *gender* studies have been examining the construction of male attributes and attitudes that are typical of certain societies and cultures at specific historical moments. Results of such studies have appeared in a number of essay collections (Kaufman 1987; Brod 1987). Other contemporary approaches criticize *gender duality*, the idea that there are only two types of encultured gender which correspond to the two biological sexes (Butler 1990); theorists and writers working in the area of gay and lesbian studies focus on the gender complexities raised by homosexual contexts and practices such as cross-dressing or transvestism. For the purposes of this book, however, the main focus will be on ideas of *gender* applied in the women's movement and in women's studies in order to understand and then undermine, or strategically exploit, the effects of gender identity in women.

The women's movement of the late 1960s and early 1970s focused on two aspects of women's difference. First, it tried to show how women's difference from men was in many ways due to the artificial behavioural stereotypes that come with gender conditioning. Since these stereotypes were artificial, they could be minimized. Second, the movement de-emphasized differences between women, stressing instead women's shared experiences, their commonality, their solidarity. In other words, it viewed gender as a form of deliberate cultural conditioning that needed to be criticized and rejected, but that also transcended individual cultures and could bond women into a political force (Eisenstein 1983). This led to the "ideological and political conviction that women were more unified by the fact of being female in a patriarchal society than [...] divided by specificities of race and class" (Eisenstein 1983:xvii). The idea of gender as a largely negative aspect of women's conditioning could thus be strategically and politically exploited to bring women together.

Gender was understood to be the basis of women's subordination in public and private life, and was viewed as an phenomenon affecting all women – in the household as well as in the workplace, everywhere from the pink-collar ghettos of the corporations, via images of women in the media, to government or educational agencies establishing policies affecting women. It was a part of everywoman's life. Activities criticizing the gendered aspects of everyday life kept the issue in the public eye; interest and support were galvanized by media events such as the disruption of the Miss America Pageant in 1968, where the trappings of stereotypical femininity – dish-cloths, steno pads, girdles and bras – were thrown into a 'Freedom Trash Can' (Morgan 1968:62-67).

The establishment of women's studies' initiatives developed from this sense of women's commonality as well as from the realization that women were excluded from large parts of public and academic life. It marked a new development toward the implantation of feminist ideas in the academy and found its justification in two factors. First, traditional claims about the 'universality' of knowledge and scholarship were untenable; second, it was precisely the gendered difference of women's lives that needed to be examined and understood. This led to women-centred perspectives which debunked claims of scholarly or political objectivity and rewrote history, literary history, sociology and psychology from women's points of view. A good example of such feminist revisionism is the critique of the student protest movements of the 1960s in France and Germany, in the USA and in Quebec's mid-1960s cultural revolution. Rather than viewing these movements as being as egalitarian as their rhetoric, feminist researchers have shown that they were to a large extent carried out on the backs of their female participants. The feminist journal from Quebec, *Québécoises deboutte!*, which was published in the early 1970s and anthologized in 1982, clearly documents the unabashed male bias of the 'Quiet Revolutionaries' (O'Leary and Toupin 1982).

While many research initiatives in women's studies have focused on the critical rewriting of received knowledge, some work has also led to positive views of women's engendered behaviour, associating women with qualities of nurturing, cooperation, ecological sensitivity as well as considerable psychological and physical strength. These views have, however, received severe criticism from within the women's movement for being essentialist and positing some kind of universal psychological essence for all women. Indeed, by the early to mid-1980s intense processes of differentiation *between* women developed, as scholars uncovered and investigated the historical and cross-cultural differences in women's lives (Rosaldo 1980; Mohanty 1984; Moraga and Anzaldúa 1983).

The realization that these differences between women were important caused some disturbance of the common ground on which ideas about gender had been founded. Nonetheless, gender as an analytical category continues to motivate researchers in diverse areas. In psychology, for example, feminist thinkers have developed the area of child psychology, taking into account the gendered differences between girls and boys and the effect they have on their development (Gilligan 1982). In literary studies, the work of hitherto neglected women writers has been unearthed, examined, translated and made available. Similarly, women's histories are being written, and account is being taken of women's contributions in the arts, in music, in philosophy, in medicine, and so on. It has become unacceptable to exclude simply on the basis of gender (or race or other factors). Research and writing that does so can no longer presume to be accurate, let alone make claims for universal applicability.

In Anglo-American contexts, gender issues have made sizeable inroads into the academic and political domains, affecting numerous social and institutional structures. Gender has come to be recognized as an important analytical category as well as a factor that has an impact on business decisions, educational institutions and governmental policies. It is recognized as a basic substructure of society that must be examined, understood and analyzed in its many forms and functions.

## Women and Language

Though the social sciences were the first to be affected by issues of gender, the term soon entered the realms of language and literature. Attention was drawn to the fact that language is not only a tool for communication but also a manipulative tool. This idea was developed by authors such as Hélène Cixous, Claudine Herrmann, Marina Yaguello, Annie Leclerc in France, Mary Daly, Kate Millett, Adrienne Rich in the United States, and Nicole Brossard, Louky Bersianik, France Théoret in Canada. The subsequent focus on the effects of 'patriarchal' language – the language forged and used by the institutions in society largely ruled by men – led to outpourings of scholarly analyses and literary texts. Some of the many questions that scholars posed and sought to answer centred around language use: How do women use language? Is their use different from men's? Do women carry out different communicative roles from those of men? Other questions focused on how gender was reflected in language: How are women and men represented in conventional language? How is women's and men's consciousness moulded through language? How is gender difference constructed and reinforced in language? Yet another cluster of questions was concerned with the ramifications of language issues in power struggles: How is power enhanced or undermined through language? How are individuals or groups manipulated by language? Does gender difference in language also mean different kinds of access to public life and influence?

There were two different approaches to questions about women and language; they could be broadly viewed as reformist and radical. The reformist approach was to view conventional language as a *symptom* of the society that spawned it, accepting it as conceivably reformable, if good intentions prevailed. The radical approach was to view conventional language as an important *cause* of women's oppression, the medium through which women were taught and came to know their subordinate place in the world (Cameron 1985). The reformist approach led to the creation of handbooks of 'non-sexist' language, language education workshops and training courses, and language planning by agencies such as the *Office de la langue française* in Quebec which has been developing gender-free job designations. The idea was to clearly represent women in language, rather than subsume them under the category 'Man'. In the radical approach, women located themselves in the role of the individual that is excluded, insulted or trivialized by conventional patriarchal language. From this perspective all of conventional language becomes a danger to women's confidence, self-esteem, psychological development and creativity, precisely because it is controlled and manipulated by 'malestream' institutions. Deborah Cameron's highly readable discussion of these issues summarizes this radical viewpoint as follows:

> The radical feminist view, then, is of women who live and speak within the confines of a man-made symbolic universe. They must cope with the disjunction between the linguistically validated male world view and their own experience, which cannot be expressed in male language. Indeed, since language determines reality, women may be alienated not only from language but also from the female experience it fails to encode. (1985:93)

This view held that language was not only a man-made artifact, but it was made to reflect men's lives, their realities, their ideas. It determined and named *men*'s realities, leaving women's realities indescribable. The only remedy could be a full-scale revamping of language so that women's specificity might be accounted for and women's development be made possible.

The remedies that were applied to patriarchal language took radical forms, triggering the earliest discussions of gender and translation. Writers took issue with standard language and criticized, rewrote or ignored dictionaries and other established reference materials. They viewed standard syntax and the established literary genres as reflecting and perpetuating patriarchal power structures. They tried to find a new language and new literary forms for women that would reflect and respond to women's realities; they began to criticize and radically change existing language so that it might be rendered useful, rather than inherently dangerous for women. As the French theorist Luce Irigaray puts it:

> Si nous continuons à nous parler le même langage, nous allons reproduire la même histoire. Recommencer les mêmes histoires. (Irigaray 1977:205)

(If we continue to speak the same language, we will reproduce the same (his)story. Repeat the same (his)stories. (my translation)

Women writers who subscribed to this position tried to get beyond the 'same language' that had been identified as detrimental to women's well-being. Throughout the 1970s women writers created experimental works in which patriarchal language became one of the main themes. In Quebec, Louky Bersianik easily demonstrated the male bias of standard French: her character l'Euguelionne, a creature who arrives on earth from outer space and describes what she finds, is amazed at the definition of *virile*. The *Petit Robert* states firstly that *virile* designates qualities typical of, even exclusive to men ("propre à l'homme"), and then goes on to list such qualities as "actif, énergique, courageux, etc." (active, energetic, courageous). L'Euguelionne is perplexed that these characteristics should be designated as exclusively male and she wonders whether women do not have such qualities. The questions raised by this kind of dictionary entry point to the underlying ideology of conventional language. Even twenty years later, the *Petit Robert* dictionary, under the entry for *femme* (woman) continues to carry the following citation from Malraux: "Une femme est AUSSI un être humain" (A woman is ALSO a human being). An interesting comment on contemporary lexicography.

While women undertook work like Bersianik's in many different languages, others focused on etymological research to reclaim words. They unearthed old or obsolete words for women's activities, or rehabilitated terms they found degraded in patriarchal usage. Mary Daly, writing in the United States in the mid-1970s, took issue with the contemporary meanings of ancient words which, in her view, are indicators of a once powerful women's culture: words such as 'hag' and 'crone' and 'spinster' have exclusively negative connotations today, yet they once referred to women who were powerful and autonomous. Daly asserts that since men are the ones who want to be powerful and autonomous, and women therefore have to be helpless and subject to men, it is in men's interest to denigrate such words. For Daly, a definition of *hag* as a "frightening or evil spirit" reveals more about those who write and publish the definition than it does about the term they purport to define. While Daly's work has been criticized for many different reasons, its tone and style of argumentation are not untypical of the period.

The idea that conventional language and its use in both public and private situations is detrimental to women had far-reaching consequences. It was explored by linguists who analyzed many Western languages in order to describe, document and combat oppressive aspects of semantics, grammar systems, proverbs, myths and metaphors. Sociolinguists studied women's silence in public situations as well as the linguistic work they do in their partnerships (Spender 1980; Tröml-Plötz 1982). Psychoanalysts and therapists such as Luce Irigaray and Julia Kristeva explored the connections between language use and women's psychological disorders and psychoses. Development workers in both developing and first world countries investigated the disproportionate cases of illiteracy or semi-literacy among women (Kaplan 1976). Others examined women's restricted access to writing, publishing, and public influence in the industrial countries (Showalter 1986). Throughout these discussions and in the ensuing publications, the issue of *gender* was a dominant aspect of the straitjacket of patriarchal language. Gender was a product of patriarchal institutions and conventional language was one of these institutions. It was employed to prescribe women's options and women's condition, and to restrict and mould women to functions in the service of 'mankind' (Thorne et al. 1983).

Creative work further stretched the bounds of language. Writers began to refer back to hundreds of precursors – famous, little-known or unknown women authors; they developed dictionaries for women (Wittig and Zeig 1981; Daly and Caputi 1987) which would supplement, if not supplant, the standard works and help create women-identified language; and they proved a powerful source of new ideas, new language and new uses for 'old' language. Their work was seldom restricted only to creative writing, however; it encompassed teaching, publishing, public lectures, playwriting and other public activities, thereby making their radical approaches to language more palatable to those who found them frustratingly esoteric and difficult. Such authors helped create a community of readers for their literary/linguistic experiments. Nicole Brossard (Quebec) is an example of an experimental author who took such an integrated approach. Her creative writing confuses the genres of poetry, prose and theory and is fairly difficult to read. Yet through her activities as a journalist, a teacher, a public speaker, an editor and anthologist, she was able to develop an international community of readers for her material. Over the course of her career, she has produced a series of books of experimental writing that provide readers and researchers with new feminist concepts, new language and new literary forms to decipher, understand and use. Her work not only seeks to dismantle the power invested in patriarchal language but also describe and develop ideas about women's utopias somewhere beyond the pernicious influence of patriarchal structures and language institutions.

It is not easy, however, to read new utopias created and described in new language with new syntactic structures. How do you read a language that tries to be innovative in its own structures and forms, and at the same time purports to describe a new (utopian) state of affairs? This is a problem that has beset radical criticisms of conventional language. Many of these texts need 'mediation' – criticism and explanation – within the source language and culture, before they can be understood. The issue has become even more complex as the women's movement has developed international dimensions; cooperative ventures between European and Anglo-American feminists and women from other parts of the world have rendered the discussion culturally and linguistically more diverse. This is the point at which translation enters and complicates the picture.

**Gender and Translation**

Translation has long served as a trope to describe what women do when they enter the public sphere: they translate their private language, their specifically female forms of discourse, developed as a result of gendered exclusion, into some form of the dominant patriarchal code. Marguerite Duras explains:

> I think "feminine literature" is an organic, translated writing ... translated from blackness, from darkness. Women have been in darkness for centuries. They don't know themselves. Or only poorly. And when women write, they translate this darkness... Men don't translate. They begin from a theoretical platform that is already in place, already elaborated. The writing of women is really translated from the unknown, like a new way of communicating rather than an already formed language. (Duras 1980:174)

Duras' comment exemplifies the view that women always have to translate when they move into the public sphere. English, French and other feminist discourses have echoed this notion of writing as an 'organic' activity during which repressed, or suppressed texts have to be drawn out of a pool of nebulous, unenunciated material and then translated into conventional forms. The idea evokes women's difficult access to conventional forms of expression and publication, and is explored at length in such books as *Häutungen* (1975) by Verena Stefan and *La Venue à l'écriture* (1977) by Hélène Cixous, Madeleine Gagnon and Annie Leclerc.

Interest in gender and translation has developed into many more directions since these texts appeared. It now ranges from issues in translation practice to translation history and criticism, to new ideas in translation theory. The following chapters develop these points.

# 2. Gender and the Practice of Translation

The work of translating in an 'era of feminism', in an era powerfully influenced by feminist thought, has had an acute effect on translation practice. First, translators have sought out contemporary women's writing in order to translate it into their own cultures. Because of the experimental nature of much of this work, they have had to deal with enormous technical challenges in the translations. Second, because the women's movement has defined language as a powerful political instrument, many women working in an 'era of feminism' also face issues of intervention and censorship in translation: When and how do politicized translators 'correct' a text? To what extent does the translator's role become overtly political? And third, the interest in a lineage of important women writers and thinkers has created an impressive corpus of translated 'lost' works; due to the fact that these texts have only now been recuperated, the work of the translator moves well beyond traditional bounds of translation and incorporates annotation and criticism.

Gender awareness in translation practice poses questions about the links between social stereotypes and linguistic forms, about the politics of language and cultural difference, about the ethics of translation, and about reviving inaccessible works for contemporary readers. It highlights the importance of the cultural context in which translation is done.

**Experimental Feminist Writing and Its Translation**

The radical feminist writing of the 1970s was experimental. It was radical insofar as it sought to undermine, subvert, even destroy the conventional everyday language maintained by institutions such as schools and universities, publishing houses and the media, dictionaries, writing manuals, and the 'great works' of literature. Feminists viewed this language as an instrument of women's oppression and subjugation which needed to be reformed, if not replaced by a new women's language. They thus took on the radical position of attacking language itself, rather than just the messages carried by the language. Although other writers at other times have seen conventional language as a dangerous instrument – the post World War II German writers in *Gruppe 47*, for example, were very wary of using conventional German after their experience of Nazi-Newspeak – gender has not often been an issue in such critiques. One rare exception is the work of the *Précieuses* of seventeenth-century France, who sought to reform the rough manners at court while also refining the French language.

Radical feminist writing in the late twentieth century has been experimental in that it explores new ground, seeking to develop new ideas and a new language for women. Writers have tried out new words, new spellings, new grammatical constructions, new images and metaphors in an attempt to get beyond the conventions of patriarchal language that, in their view, determine to a large extent what women can think and write. The theory is that the language women have at their disposal will influence their creativity, affecting their ability to think in revolutionary terms and their capacity to produce new work. Verena Stefan, whose book *Häutungen* (1975) became the most influential radical feminist text written in German, expresses her position as a woman in conventional language as follows:

> Language fails me as soon as I try to speak of new experiences. Supposedly new experiences that are cast in the same old language cannot really be new. (tr. 1978/1994:53)

Experiments have blossomed in every Western European and North American country, and in all languages. Yet although the theories about women's oppression through language are largely similar, the practical applications differ greatly. This is not surprising, given the fact that writers are deconstructing different languages as well as different cultures, which require feminist attention in different places.

Nicole Brossard (Quebec) published a number of books that fit this radical deconstructive mode during the 1970s and early 1980s. Her book *L'Amèr, ou le chapitre effrité* (1977) takes as one of its themes 'the patriarchal mother' and examines it in highly experimental prose poetry. The patriarchal mother is the woman reduced to reproduction, the woman whose creativity and individuality is suffocated by this forced, unrecognized labour, and who is prone to suffocating her own children as a result. Brossard's title *L'Amèr* is a neologism that contains at least three terms in French: *mère* (mother), *mer* (sea), and *amer* (bitter). It represents the author's preoccupation with motherhood as a bitter and embittering experience, and reflects one of the important images of feminist thinking that links women to water, to the cyclical and fluid nature of the sea. Similarly, Brossard's neologism *mourriture*, used to describe what such women do or give to their children, combines the words *nourriture* (food), *pourrir* (to rot) and *mourir* (to die), thus connecting nurture, putrefaction and death in such a way that the result deconstructs ideas about women's special nurturing qualities.

Brossard's approach to linguistic deconstruction is often, though not exclusively, based on puns that play on the fact that many words have similar sounds in French. Mary Daly, an American theologian and radical feminist writer, also works with puns but extends her attack on patriarchal language into the history of words. She is concerned with the way words that were once important to women, or that once expressed women's historical power and autonomy have been degraded in patriarchy; she ceaselessly tries to revitalize such words or create new ones for use in radical feminism. More lucid than Brossard, she warns her readers that this work on language is hard work. A footnote in the preface of her influential book *Gyn/Ecology. A Metaethics of Radical Feminism* reads:

> This book contains Big Words [...] for it is written for big, strong women, out of respect for strength. Moreover, I've made some of them up. Therefore, it may be a stumbling block both to those who choose downward mobility of the mind and therefore hate Big Words, and to those who choose upward mobility and therefore hate New/Old Words, that is Old words that become New when their ancient ("obsolete") gynocentric meanings are unearthed. Hopefully, it will be a useful pathfinder for the *multiply mobile*: the movers, the weavers, the Spinners. (Daly 1978:xiv)

Daly highlights the importance she places on linguistic innovation ('New Words') and on the renewal and rehabilitation of gynocentric terms ('Old Words') that have been given derogatory meanings in patriarchy. But she also calls upon her readers to participate and flatters them into doing so: the book is written for 'big strong women' who are 'multiply mobile'.

This excerpt demonstrates a different kind of punning from that used by Brossard in *L'Amèr*. Daly's terms 'big strong woman' and 'multiply mobile' pick up on American terminology based on cultural rather than linguistic phenomena. It is probably not too much of a generalization to say that American girls of the 1960s and 1970s were socialized to be 'Daddy's little girl' or 'little lady', to be under the care of 'big strong men'. Daly turns this usage around, surprising the reader with a new combination and undermining the idea of women as helpless or incompetent 'girls'. Similarly, the play on 'upward', 'downward', and 'multiply mobile' picks up on contemporary American usage that normally uses it for the jockeying that goes on for social position. Again, the term is revamped to refer to feminist consciousness and a willing-ness to accept challenges and learn.

While the deconstruction of individual words, syntax and other for-mal elements has been an important aspect of experimental feminist writing, the female body has played an important thematic role. At the root of much feminist work is the recuperation of the objectified, ob-scured, vilified or domesticated female body. This is a body that has been depersonalized by patriarchy, that offers services in return for its maintenance, while at the same time maintaining the system that subju-gates it. This body is, however, also the source of women's creative energy, a largely unknown entity that has long been silenced and needs to be written. In "The Laugh of the Medusa", the first text by the French writer Hélène Cixous to be translated into English, the author writes:

> Women must write through their bodies, they must invent the im-pregnable language that will wreck partitions, classes and rhetorics, regulations and codes, they must submerge, cut through, get beyond the ultimate reserve/discourse ... (Cixous 1975; tr. 1976:886)

But how does one 'write through a body'? And for that matter, how does one translate the experiments in language that have been produced in response to these feminist ideas?

*Translating the Body*

When women 'write the female body' they write on a subject that has hith-erto been described in terms of the stereotypes of the lover ('whore'), the devoted and unsexed mother, or the untouchable Holy Virgin, as the Québécois play, *Les Fées ont soif* (1979) by Denise Boucher makes clear. Feminist writers have identified sexuality as the factor underlying these stereotypes, and have responded by breaking open these stereotypes and moving beyond these clichés. Women's sexuality and women's eroticism, described from a woman's point of view, have become a preferred area of experimentation in feminist writing. Writers have looked for and developed vocabulary for censored or denigrated parts of the female anatomy and tried to create erotic writing that appeals to women. They have responded to the challenge to 'tenter l'érotique', to attempt and tempt the erotic.

French language writers have been particularly innovative and bold in this regard. This tendency may be partly due to the sexualized vo-cabulary of psychoanalysis and literary criticism, where terms such as *jouissance* and *invagination* are not unusual. *Jouissance* has a number of meanings ranging from enjoyment to pleasure to sexual pleasure to orgasm, while *invagination* refers to the penetration of one text by any number of other, earlier or contemporary texts. Translating this French 'body work' into English causes distinct problems of word choice and opens translators' eyes to the limitations of their own languages. It also raises issues of self-censorship and 'decorum', for where one linguistic group may focus on 'writing the body' as a means of making political progress, another may be averse, even unable, to make a link between erotic writing and politics. Indeed, the entire semantic field around issues of sexuality has caused serious problems for translators.

Susanne de Lotbinière-Harwood (1991) has addressed the issue in a number of ways, deriving her examples from translations of Brossard's work in French and Gail Scott's in English. She takes the word *cyprine* from Brossard's *Sous la langue* (1987) to demonstrate the difficulty. *Cyprine* in French means female sexual secretions (de Lotbinière-Harwood 1991:145ff). The term has existed in French for some time, occurring in Baudelaire's *Fleurs du mal* and in work by lesbian and feminist writers of the 1970s. However, it is not in any dictionary, because, says de Lotbinière-Harwood, "lexicographers don't want to give women access to this word" (ibid:145). Nor does it exist in English; in English "we have no word, no word but wet" (ibid:147). De Lotbinière-Harwood's solution is to research and refer to the Greek etymology of *cyprine* and create an English version 'cyprin'. But the new word needed accounting for in the chapbook in which Brossard's text and her translation appeared; this meant assigning one page for the translator's note, which reads

> Female sexual secretion. From the French *cyprine* [fr. Gk Cyprus, birth place of Aphrodite]. We are proposing *cyprin* for English usage.

In this case, the translator's challenge, discussed at some length in her writings, led to the creation of a neologism. Its positioning on a page of its own, its discussion in public lectures and writing – in other words, the 'account' she has given of it – have further drawn attention both to the 'sanitized' aspects of the English language and the effects gender-awareness in translation can produce.

In another example, de Lotbinière-Harwood emphasizes the need to reclaim the term *con* in French, where it has come to refer to "un gars au comportement débile" (an obnoxious, cretinous male) (1991:64-65).

The issue arose in her translation of Gail Scott's book *Heroine* into French, where the question 'I wonder about the smell of cunt' had to be rendered 'je me demande ce que sent le con d'une femme'. The specification 'd'une femme' was necessary since it could otherwise have referred to the smell of an idiotic male. In the translator's view, the need to specify this indicates the extent to which the terms for women's sexual body have been thoroughly colonized by male use and abuse. The work of reclaiming some of this derogatory vocabulary and developing new terms is also the work of the translator. In this case, the translator could have avoided the issue by translating 'ce que sent le sexe d'une femme', thus following the usage proposed in the *Petit Robert* dictionary. However, since the English sentence is a daring provocation, de Lotbinière-Harwood wanted to take the same risk, and use the term 'con' for its transgressive value. Her view that 'translation in the feminine is a political act, and an act of women's solidarity' (1991:65) underlies this transgressive, aggressive approach.

The problem of word choice has been addressed in other contexts as well, notably in cases where the English translation demonstrates an insufficient knowledge of female biology. Godard (1984:13) gives the example of the phrase 'la perte blanche' in a text by Nicole Brossard being translated as 'white loss', and thus missing the alternate meaning of 'discharge', i.e. bodily secretions. A related issue comes up in the discussion about the different English versions of Brossard's 'Ce soir j'entre dans l'histoire sans relever ma jupe'. Brossard is referring to a woman's participation in public life as an author, rather than as a stereotypical female, here as a sexually available 'lover'. The line is from the play, *La nef des sorcières* (1976), translated as *A Clash of Symbols* (Gaboriau 1979), in which a number of figures of women, symbolizing various roles women play, present themselves. The translation, produced for performance on stage, was, "tonight I shall step into history without opening my legs" (Gaboriau 1979:35). It was acclaimed as being particularly effective despite the fact that it mistranslates, and overstates what Brossard, one of the participating authors, actually wrote. The translation works dramatically, and strikes the listening audience more forcefully than would the more careful version, 'tonight I shall enter history without lifting up my skirt'. Further, the reference to 'opening my legs' carries on into the next line, 'I step into history opening my mouth not my legs', i.e. speaking and making myself heard.

While it is difficult to negotiate the gap between the coarse and the clinical terms for women's sexual bodies, the more general term, 'jouissance', has also caused considerable debate. Defined as 'sexual pleasure, bliss, rapture' in the anthology *New French Feminisms* (Marks & de Courtivron 1980:36), it is translated throughout the anthology as 'sexual pleasure'. Yet *jouissance* also means 'enjoyment' or 'pleasure' and can refer to many kinds of enjoyment, including its use in the legal sense 'enjoyment of good health'. When it is translated exclusively as 'sexual pleasure', the stress is placed on the daring, new sexual component. When it is not translated, but left in French and annotated instead, attention is also drawn to its exotic, perhaps 'non-English' qualities. This has been viewed negatively as a sign of "dismissive American coy righteousness" (Freiwald 1991:63) since the translator thereby avoids addressing the polysemic, sexual component. On the other hand, it can also be coded as a positive aspect of a translation that allows an English work to retain a French 'accent' (de Lotbinière-Harwood 1991:150).

Discussions between French and English women have often focused on the issue of eroticism and its terminology (Freiwald 1991), on the problem of women's empowerment on the one hand and their alienation from each other on the other; debates have raged about where to locate references to women's bodies and their sexuality on the sliding scale between two extreme poles. And translation has not always been a solution, as a discussion published in *Yale French Studies* in 1981 shows. Viewing translations of works by French feminist writers as mediations that make the 'other' culture appear both "fascinating and fearful, and extremely glamorous", Sandra Gilbert, one of the discussants, calls for "mediations of mediations" (1981:6-7). She wants explanations of the translations, further cultural material that place these texts into their philosophical, literary and social contexts. Gail Scott, a bilingual Canadian writer, has summarized this issue of contexts in vivid terms, paralleling the gap between English and French feminist discourses to the gap between Protestant anglophone moral rigidity and the relative moral ease provided by the French Roman Catholic confessional (Scott 1989). There are doubtless other causes at work. The translation of feminist writing of the gendered body is one area where the limits of language and the constraints imposed by culture have led to a certain disruption of feminist ideas about women's solidarity and their shared fate in patriarchy.

*Translating Puns on Cultural References*

Puns are linked to pain; "puns are punishment" writes Suzanne Jill Levine (1991:13). She makes this comment with reference to her work on texts by Cuban writers in exile. Exile is pain, too. For 1970s feminist writers such as Mary Daly or France Théoret, women live in exile in patriarchal language; punning expresses their pain, but it is also a way to fight back. Translating puns, on the other hand, has proven to be a form of 'pun-ishment' in much feminist work.

Mary Daly's book *Gyn/Ecology* (1978) is full of wordplay on aspects of American culture; she invents neologisms such as 'the-rapist', 'bore-ocracy' and the 'Totaled woman' to refer to more or less familiar ideas and then to undermine them with humour, irony, and anger. The implication is that therapists work for patriarchy, keeping women in check by the age-old method of sexual violence or the threat of it; the bureaucracy bores people into passivity and exists to maintain its boring self; the 'Totaled woman' is the finished product of fashion-magazine designs but is closer to being 'totaled' the way a car is after a crash. These and many other of Daly's puns work remarkably well in English. In the German translation, however, they are the source of serious problems.

For one thing the cultural situations are different. Therapies of various kinds were not as widespread a social phenomenon in 1970s Germany as they were in the USA, and the issue of sexual and emotional abuse of women patients by their psychotherapists had had no exposure at all. This issue has only begun to be addressed in Germany in the 1990s. More problematic, however, is the fact that the linguistic aspects of the puns just don't work in German. In German 'therapist' is *Therapeut* and 'rapist' is *Vergewaltiger*. The same problem arises with the 'Totaled woman'. The 'total' fashion look might translate as *ganzheitlich weiblich* or *durchgestylt*, while a car that is 'totaled' has suffered a *Totalschaden*. Again there is no immediate linguistic relationship that can be exploited. The same goes for Daly's term 'womb-tomb' for 'spacecraft'. The German translator is hard put to find something as succinct and homophonic. Her translation *Mutterschoß-Grabstätte* is a literal rendering.

While such difficulties arise in all wordplay translation, they have a particular effect in the translation of feminist experimental writing. When Daly's translator, Erika Wisselinck, resorts to literal translation in the 'womb-tomb' example because she wants to stress the meaning of the feminist text, she avoids the wordplay and misses out on the humorous, lightening role that puns have. This renders the translation more weighty and serious than the source text. Literal translation stems from the desire not to lose even a scrap of information or connotation, and it is often complemented by explanatory translator's notes. These make the translation heavy reading material, but are, at the same time, a factor of the cultural context in which the translation is completed. The translator sees herself working for the cause of the women's movement;

in this work, she regularly oversteps the bounds of invisibility that traditionally define her role.

*Translating Experiments with Language*

Feminist experiments with language have raised another set of problems for the translator. When the grammar of a language such as French dictates that nouns, adjectives and participles need to be gender-identified, feminist writers can subvert this gender requirement and the symbolic system that underlies it by applying the grammar system differently. This could mean feminizing words to give them new meanings, as in Brossard's 'matern*ell*', 'homoindividu*ell*', 'essentiel*le*' or her term '*ma* continent', which are all feminized neologisms. Similarly, when the syntax of a language or its conventions of style are too restrictive for women's new vision, the writer can change it. The outcome has been described as follows with regard to the work of Nicole Brossard:

> Brossard disrupts these power relationships in language by challenging our normal expectations about punctuation, spacing and typography. Attempting to subvert our *passive* consumption of novel or poem, she blurs grammatical constructions, introduces blanks, gaps, ruptures, deconstructing the text so that meaning is negotiated through a perpetual process of interaction. (Godard 1984:15)

Yet the place where power relations are disrupted in French may not correspond to the spots where they need to or can be disrupted in English, German or any other language. Moreover, the 'perpetual process of interaction' that reading such a text implies is in some danger of being lost in translation, where the translator makes definitive language choices which may render the text less ambiguous.

Howard Scott has provided a good example of a translation problem created by wordplay on grammar. In a section of *L'Euguélionne* by Louky Bersianik (1976), there is a passage on the politics of abortion; the following line occurs:

Le ou la coupable doit être punie.

The additional *e* on the past participle *puni* indicates it is the woman who is punished for abortion. But this subtlety doesn't transfer smoothly to English, which lacks gender agreement. Scott's solution supplements the lack in English and reads :

The guilty one must be punished, whether she is a man or a woman.

Although the past participle is left untouched in the English version, the legal disjunction that Bersianik is pointing to in the French is clear in 'whether *she* is a man or a woman' (Scott 1984:35; my emphasis).

This is one case where the play with the silent *e* in French can be compensated elsewhere in the text. Other terms such as *essentielle* which is feminized, or *laboratoir* which is masculinized to mark the absence of the feminine, are either left in the original language and footnoted or are lost in that particular application. Barbara Godard, one of Brossard's translators, has noted that to compensate for such losses, she has used other wordplay that might be more familiar or accessible to English readers; for instance, 're(her)ality' for *réalité* or 'reading/deliring' for *dé-lire* (Godard 1984, 1986, 1991a).

Much of the punning on language in feminist writing also works through sound associations and alliterations, as in Mary Daly's 'womb-tomb'. Brossard's text *Sous la langue* (1987) was written to be read aloud at an evening of experimental poetry reading. It contains lines like the following:

> Fricatelle ruisselle essentielle aime-t-elle dans le touche à tout qui arrondit les seins la rondeur douce des bouches ou l'effet qui la déshabille?

The word/sound *elle* at the end of the first four words both reinforces the feminine context of the text and creates the neologisms *essentielle* and *fricatelle*, a variation on *fricarelle* (1930s slang for the sound made by thighs rubbing together). Further, the 'oo' sound connoting physical pleasure is stressed in the phrases *touche à tout* and *rondeur douce des bouches ou* ..., enhancing meaning with sound. In *Under Tongue*, the English translation of Brossard (1987), Susanne de Lotbinière-Harwood focuses on the *elle* endings and finds a way to fit in the pronoun 'she':

> Does she frictional she fluvial she essential does she in the all-embracing touch that rounds the breasts love the mouths' soft roundness or the effect undressing her?

The translator here pays less attention to the meaning of the words than to their sounds. Even the repetition of the soft vowel sound is approximated, though it comes across as the English 'ow' ('rounds', 'mouths', 'roundness'). In her translation of Brossard's *Amantes* (Brossard 1980, tr. 1987), Godard also emphasizes sound associations in English that may create an effect similar to the French puns based on homophones. She seems unworried by what might appear to be the resulting mistranslation, since in certain cases she is deliberately translating on the phonemic level.

So, what has experimental feminist writing meant for translation practice? Most importantly, it has foregrounded the issue of gender in language and caused translators to respond to the resulting technical and theoretical challenges. When confronted with texts full of wordplay and fragmented syntax, translators have had to develop creative methods similar to those of the source-text writers; they have had to go beyond translation to supplement their work, making up for the differences between various patriarchal languages by employing wordplay, grammatical dislocations and syntactic subversion in other places in their texts. In the translation of work that 'writes the body', they have dealt with the fact that in many languages words need to be created or recuperated to name and describe culturally taboo aspects of the female body. The practical work of translating experimental feminist writing has thus politicized numerous translators. Much of the theoretical discussion on gender and translation has been initiated by women translators first faced with these texts.

## Interventionist Feminist Translation

Just as translators may develop political sympathies for experimental feminist writing and then transfer those attitudes to their work, so translators who are already politicized may take offence at texts that are unpalatable or politically unacceptable. Like Peter Newmark, who recently argued that translators should 'correct' source material in the name of the "moral facts as known" (1991:46), a concept he simplifies with the term "truth" (ibid:1), feminist translators 'correct' texts that they translate in the name of feminist 'truths'. Over the past decade a number of women translators have assumed the right to query their source texts from a feminist perspective, to intervene and make changes when the texts depart from this perspective. Drawing attention to the political clout they personally assign to language and to the impact of a translator's politics, they openly intervene in their texts. Overt interventionism by translators is rather controversial, however, since translators are normally expected, even assumed, to keep their politics out of their work. Yet, as translation historians know, deliberate changes have often been made in rewritten texts, and frequently in the name of some ideology.

A good example of a covertly interventionist translation is the East German translation of Christa Wolf's *Der Geteilte Himmel* (1963), published as *Divided Heaven* in East Berlin in 1965. Massive changes were made in the work without any indication or explanation; among other things, a stream-of-consciousness narration by a young woman hesitatingly coming to terms with the new socialist Germany and the Wall it had just raised was turned into a thin prose account of the plot, written entirely in the third person. And the woman protagonist's hesitations were largely deleted. Critic Katharina von Ankum (1993) has speculated on the 'patriarchal' element of developing socialism that may have led to these modifications.

When feminist translators intervene in a text for political reasons, they draw attention to their action. In so doing, they demonstrate how easily misogynist aspects of patriarchal language can be dismantled once they have been identified. They also demonstrate their decision-making powers.

*Translating Machismo*

For Carol Maier and Suzanne Jill Levine the work of translating Cuban or South American male writers has repeatedly raised issues of sexism. Maier's discussion of the problem focuses on the sexist content of poems by Cuban poet Octavio Armand. The works in question refer to birth, in particular the image of his birth "from my father's womb" Maier writes:

> I was prompted to review both the mother's role in Armand's work and my own relationship to that role. As I read back through his poems and essays to 'inventory' the presence of both parents, what I found was the continual appearance of a strong father and the faint trace of a mother who is indeed little more than a shadow. (1985:5)

The fact that Maier's work is carried out in "an era of feminism" (ibid) prompts her to sift through Armand's father/mother images, and to enquire about her own response to them; this academic and cultural context encourages her to express her criticism and her standpoint as a translator. She goes on to find that while in Armand's writing the father "makes all phases of life possible", the mother is "an absence, a smudge" (ibid). She also locates subtle indications of misogyny in the way Armand describes the link between language, his 'mother tongue', and his anxiety about its capacity to express what he wants to say. He often casts this uncertainty in negative images associated with women: the tongue can be "filed, combed and polished", it is sharp, forked, deceitful, it is a "mistress of both lips who is guilty of giving birth to din and confusion and to expression that petrifies...." (ibid). And the poet's heart is burned by the "round red fruit" of female treachery.

Having uncovered a system of sexist thinking and metaphorics in her author, Maier enquires about her own intentions in translating texts that

> robbed a mother of her speech without even giving her a chance to speak for herself, likening her to a tongue but denying her a body, referring to her birthday but denying her presence at the poet's birth. (ibid:6)

For Maier, the issue of intention becomes entangled with her identity as a North American woman translator. The process of confronting Armand's texts has put her earlier 'automatic and submissive' identification with the author into question. She cannot reproduce the sexism of this Cuban male writer; she writes: "I felt anger. I wanted the mother to be present, wanted her and her mothers to be signing their names along with the father and grandfathers" (ibid:7).

Suzanne Jill Levine experiences similar difficulties when she translates work by Guillermo Cabrera Infante, whose writing she describes as "oppressively male" (1983/1992:85), narcissistic, misogynist, and manipulative. Indeed, a number of the other Latin American writers she has translated, such as Manuel Puig and Severo Sarduy, also exploit the archetypal versions of "Woman [as] Other: either idealized or degraded" (Levine 1991:181). Infante, for example, uses language to obscure or "mock women and their words" (Levine 1983/1992:82) and all these writers, Levine writes, use images of women to express "language's slippery strategies" (1991:182). In other words, using metaphors and images referring more or less negatively to women, these writers express their own uncertainty in language, their distrust of official language, and at the same time their fear and distrust of women. Levine asks similar questions to those of Maier: "Where does this leave a woman as translator of such a book? Is she not a double betrayer, to play Echo to this Narcissus, repeating the archetype once again?"(1983/1992:83).

Levine's partial answer to this question is to point to the changes she makes in the text. Yet the examples are sparse. She gives one clear instance where she is able to undermine the narcissistic posturing of the

26

narrator and recuperate some aspect of women's strength. She translates his "jaded" statement "no one man can rape a woman" as "no wee
man can rape a woman" (1983/1992:83). The source text implies that
women are willing rape victims; Levine undermines this 'patriarchal'
notion by replacing 'one' with 'wee'. When both the Spanish and English texts are available, the alliterative aspects of 'one' and 'wee' are a
source of amusement that enhances Levine's obvious risk-taking. Maier's
work is equally sparse on examples: she too says more about her discomfort at the misogyny of the source text than about her actual
interventions in it.

Both Maier and Levine react to the stereotypical postures of authority assumed by or assigned to male figures in the texts and the
archetypal terms and images used for women. Yet neither translator
considers censorship, i.e. non-translation, an option. Their solution is
to undermine the text here and there, reinstating the mother or diminish-
ing the man, but keeping the text available for readers.

*Assertive Feminist Translation*

The tone is less conciliatory in work by Susanne de Lotbinière-Harwood
(1991), which appeared only a few years later in the linguistically more
politicized context of Quebec. She offers no excuses or justifications
for feminist intervention in texts, but an abundance of compelling reasons. De Lotbinière-Harwood openly practises feminist translation and
clearly situates herself as a participant in the discourses of Quebec's
experimental *écriture au féminin*, as a politicized, feminist subject. For
her, no act of writing or translation is neutral and *réécriture au féminin*
(rewriting in the feminine) is a conscious act that

> met cartes sur table dès le début. Son projet est de faire entrer la
> conscience féministe dans l'activité traductive. [...] la traduction
> se présente comme une activité politique visant à faire apparaître
> et vivre les femmes dans la langue et dans le monde. (ibid:11)

> puts its cards on the table from the very beginning. Its project is to
> imbue translation praxis with feminist consciousness [...] transla-
> tion thus becomes a political activity that has the objective of
> making women visible and resident in language and society. (my
> translation)

In her view, issues of sexism or women's silencing need not only be pointed out, they need to be solved with deliberate feminist intervention that redresses the imbalance and places women directly into the language. And censorship, if only for reasons of the translator's mental health, is definitely an option; on this topic de Lotbinière-Harwood describes her debut as a translator of Quebec rock lyrics by Lucien Francoeur:

> Francoeur was the first and last male poet I translated. During the three years I spent on his poetry, I realized with much distress that my translating voice was being distorted into speaking in the masculine. Forced by the poems' stance, by language, by my profession, to play the role of male voyeur. As if the only speaking place available, and the only audience possible, were male-bodied. I became very depressed around meaning. (1995:64)

De Lotbinière-Harwood's decision to translate only women authors from that point on may be decried as "the paradox of censorship in the name of feminism" (Maier 1985:4), analogous to the rejection suffered traditionally by women writers in patriarchy. For her, it is a question of self-preservation; and for readers it may be an indication of the extent to which the translator's female identity and feminist subjectivity enters into her work.

A good example of this assertive, interventionist translation praxis is de Lotbinière-Harwood's translation of 'generic' writing, writing in French that uses the 'universal' forms of the French language and grammar, ostensibly including references to women in the predominantly masculine forms of words and gender agreements. Pursuing the objective of "making women visible and resident in language and society", she deliberately feminizes an entire English translation of a text written in 'generic' French. Further, she includes an introduction to the work and copious translator's footnotes to ensure that readers are aware of the changes she has made.

The source text in question is *Lettres d'une autre* by Lise Gauvin (de Lotbinière-Harwood 1989), a collection of letters to a friend abroad by a 'Persian' woman visiting Quebec. The epistolary format allows the author to maintain the fiction of the foreigner observing and commenting on Quebec realities of the 1980s, and filtering them through an outsider's eyes. In the translator's preface, Lise Gauvin is presented as a feminist, and given that the exchange of letters is between two women one might expect a certain amount of feminist complicity or collusion. Yet there is still much room for feminist intervention in the translation.

De Lotbinière-Harwood explains in her preface 'About the *her* in other':

> Dear reader,
> Just a few words to let you know that this translation is a rewrit-
> ing in the feminine of what I originally read in French. I don't
> mean content. Lise Gauvin is a feminist, and so am I. But I am not
> her. She wrote in the generic masculine. My translation practice
> is a political activity aimed at making language speak for women.
> So my signature on a translation means: this translation has used
> every possible feminist translation strategy to make the feminine
> visible in language. Because making the feminine visible in lan-
> guage means making women seen and heard in the real world.
> Which is what feminism is all about. (de Lotbinière-Harwood
> 1989:9)

This assertive tone contrasts with both Maier's and Levine's. De
Lotbinière-Harwood does not mitigate her interventionist measures with
explanations about her discomfort or dismay at patriarchal language:
she assumes the right to change what she cannot approve of. Further,
she categorically states her political position and defines translation as
a political practice.

In the rest of the preface de Lotbinière-Harwood gives examples of
the types of changes she makes. The most controversial of these is also
the subject of the first translator's footnote. She translates *Québécois*,
the adjective designating the population of Québec, into English as
*Québécois-e-s*. She thus takes the French masculine plural adjective
(which supposedly includes all the female inhabitants of Quebec) and
uses a source language feminist neologism, which specifically adds the
female component with the hyphen plus the silent *e*, to translate the
term into English. The English text is thus punctuated with a feminized
Québécois neologism, described in the first footnote as the "non-sexist
grammatical transcription comprising both genders" (1989:25). Other
changes explained in the preface include the disruption of normal English word order: she uses *her and his* and *women and men* to avoid
'generic malespeak'. She makes the male or female referent of an ambiguous French pronoun such as *ils* (they) clear, and uses translational
or graphic devices to undermine such "absurd" terms as *la victoire de
l'homme* (mankind's victory) or a reference to women as *maîtres de la
cuisine*.

Interestingly, de Lotbinière-Harwood acknowledges that this type
of translation is possible because of the contemporary cultural context:

a feminist translator working on a less radical but still feminist source text for publication with an anglophone feminist publishing house. This convergence of political perspectives is typical of the kind generated by 1970s and 1980s feminist activism. Questions of gender difference are easily brought to bear on translation in such a political climate.

## Recovering Women's Works 'Lost' in Patriarchy

Feminists point out that the patriarchal canon has traditionally defined aesthetics and literary value in terms that privileged work by male writers to the detriment of women writers; as a result, much writing by women has been 'lost'. This is true of the twentieth century, even though recent feminist activism has integrated many women writers into literary histories. It is more particularly true of women writers from earlier periods, whose works need to be unearthed by literary historians and read again by literary critics. Translation has begun to play an important role in making available the knowledge, experiences and creative work of many of these earlier women writers. Numerous publications of such work have appeared in translation in recent years, often accompanied by academic essays contextualizing the source texts and discussing some of the issues these translations raise. Diane Rayor's collection of lyric poetry by women poets of ancient Greece (1991) is one such book; Helen Dendrinou Kolias' English version of the autobiography of Elisavet Moutzan-Martinengou (Kolias 1989), a nineteenth-century upper-class woman from the Greek island of Zakynthos, is another; and the numerous anthologies of women's writing in translation, for example the two volume *Women Writing in India* (Tharu & Lalita 1991/1993), are further examples of the productive translation effects of gender-awareness.

The project of recovering 'lost' women's knowledge and influence is clearly pursued in the anthology, *Translating Slavery. Gender and Race in French Women's Writing, 1783-1823* (Kadish & Massardier-Kenney 1994). The anthology assembles, translates and discusses the works of three late eighteenth- and early nineteenth-century French women, who were prominent public figures in their day. It focuses on their attitudes to race, and in particular, slavery. The source texts by Olympe de Gouges, Germaine de Staël and Claire de Duras are translated and located in their historical and cultural context. They are accompanied by commentaries in which the editors and translators discuss why these texts have been ignored or denigrated by scholars working in the patriarchal tradition, and present their arguments for reviving these works. One of the most important arguments is that a lineage of intellectual women who resisted the norms and values of the societies in which they lived needs to be unearthed and established. In this case, abolitionist writing by such women needs to be reinstated, preserved and emphasized, since women of later eras will otherwise lose sight of the achievements of their forerunners. This is clearly a project that inscribes itself in the work of recovering knowledge that has been 'lost' in patriarchy.

But the project also has other objectives. Specifically, it presents English versions of abolitionist texts previously left largely untranslated. It thus fills a gap in our knowledge about anti-slavery writings around the time of the French Revolution and during the Napoleonic period. It demonstrates and comments on the interplay of abolitionist politics, gender and translation in Europe over the fifty years from 1783 to 1823, emphasizing the role women played in abolitionist activism through writing and translation. Just as important, however, the anthology acknowledges and addresses the historical, cultural and discursive differences that exist between the eighteenth/nineteenth-century texts and their contemporary twentieth-century readers and translators. It thus points to the relative nature of aesthetic and intellectual criteria and discusses the problems that these pose for translators. The anthology makes translation its central focus and openly discusses the ideological aspects that shape every translated text.

The central premise of the *Translating Slavery* anthology is that women figured as important thinkers and writers on abolitionism in the eighteenth and nineteenth centuries in Europe and North America. Their attitudes and texts derived from and fostered ideas that had developed in Restoration England and the French Enlightenment periods; texts from those periods had been translated and had in turn inspired other political and fictional works. Aphra Behn's *Oronoko* (1696) and its French translation *Oronooko* (1745) mark an early point in this development, while Harriet Beecher Stowe's *Uncle Tom's Cabin* (1852) – published in two French versions in 1853 – marks a later moment. In between lie the works of Olympe de Gouges, Germaine de Staël and Claire de Duras.

The translations in *Translating Slavery* follow the re-constructive strategies evident in the accompanying essays. They use various means to recover and emphasize the way their authors integrate ideas about race and gender. Maryann DeJulio, the translator of Olympe de Gouges' play *L'esclavage des noirs*, for instance, describes how she exploits the gendered aspects of language "by feminizing all possessive adjectives and pronouns that relate to abstract notions of justice and compassion" (in Kadish & Massardier-Kenney 1994:127) and

31

by feminiz[ing] the generic term "author", along with the fruits of authorial productivity ('her writings'), in order to strike a clearer difference between Gouges, the writer whose gender here allies her with representations of virtue and goodness; and men, even men of color, when they seek to imitate tyrants or are condemned to servitude by their "Fatherland". (ibid:127)

De Julio participates in Gouges' identification of women with "representations of virtue and goodness", maintaining that the text's "emotional poignancy" warrants such interpretation and translation.

Other translators intervene in places where female heroines are too sentimental or melodramatic for late twentieth-century tastes, displaying a 'corrective' tendency reminiscent of de Lotbinière-Harwood's work on 'generic' language. Both translators and editors embed their work in a rhetoric of women's solidarity across the centuries. Typically, they link women with anti-slavery sentiments, stressing the connections their authors make between the "oppression of Africans and women by the French male patriarchy" (Kadish & Massardier-Kenney 1994:144) and defending their authors against charges of "Franco-centrism" (ibid:142ff, Staël), mediocrity (ibid:79ff, Gouges), or subtle racist prejudice (Duras). They thus seek to make accessible and credible the work of women long ignored in patriarchal scholarship, and in so doing create links between writing, translation politics, and issues of culture and gender.

*Further Corrective Measures*

The special cultural situation that allows feminist translation projects to flourish is acknowledged in the preface to *Translating Slavery*. The context of a university press, a sympathetic audience, women writers and women translators have made it possible to make "the feminine visible in the text and valorize it" (Massardier-Kenney 1994:17). Yet in order to 'valorize' eighteenth-century texts for late twentieth-century readers a number of important changes have had to be made. Women writers of the late eighteenth century can not be directly transferred into our late twentieth-century ideas about oppositional activity; the translators' desire to "empower the female characters dictated a number of their choices"(1994:17).

Here, then, an oppositional feminine discourse of the late eighteenth century is revived but also confronted with the expectations of politicized women of the twentieth century, and brought into contact with ideas that have developed 200 years later. This has doubtless been the case with many translations in which the source and translated text production dates lie so far apart. But contrary to many such cases, this anthology openly acknowledges the process of adjustment:

> the collaborators of this volume wish to come out into the open, to move, so to speak, from the preface to the surface, to face and perhaps "deface" these texts in a movement which acknowledges that translation practice is always a practice of a "theory" or a working out of an ideological position, but also that translation theory inevitably emerges out of a specific practice. (Massardier-Kenney 1994:12)

In this case, the specific practices have to do with North American work on gender and race in literature. For example, from the perspective of literary history, this translation practice revives and makes available texts written by 'oppositional' women of earlier centuries; it posits educated women as having been and continuing to be particularly concerned with the oppressed and the marginalized. From the perspective of contemporary discourses on gender and its effects on translation, these translations emphasize women's 'resistance', while also showing and discussing women's differences; for the African-American translator de Staël's text is reminiscent of the racist attitudes she grew up with in the USA, while the European translator is not at all sensitive to this aspect of de Staël's *Mirza*. Finally, from the perspective of the discourses on racial difference, these texts raise the issue of colonialist translation; at one point there is even a debate about whether some of the original French ought to be rendered in Wolof, one of the languages of Cameroon, in order to rectify the colonialist stance of the source text.

The interventionist aspect is perhaps most clearly visible where the eighteenth-century texts do not correspond with twentieth-century values. For example, Germaine de Staël's text *Mirza* poses specific problems with regard to gender: its main female character, Mirza, is a black woman. In order to demonstrate her nobility of character, and thus counteract some of the racist thinking in Europe, Staël gave her a very literary, refined way of speaking. The translator, wishing to make that voice meaningful for contemporary readers has made changes. She explains:

> I was a little annoyed by the romantic excesses of Mirza. I must say, that in my translation I tried to soften the excesses and wanted to valorize her speech. I wanted to make sure that people reading only the English would get from the text a sense of the power of that voice, as opposed to the quaint or romantic. (ibid:175)

This difference in voice is often an issue in translation. One historical period uses a different discourse from another, and as in this case, can be embarrassed or annoyed by inappropriate (here, flowery) speech. To change this voice in the name of feminist ideology is to take the irritation a step further, and intervene.

A similar problem occurs in the work *Ourika* by Claire de Duras. The translation "heightens the eloquence of the black female character" (Kadish & Massardier-Kenney 1994:16) in order to comply with the feminist wish to make women's voices heard. But certain types of women's voices are more valuable than others, and some require modernization as in the previous example, or even embellishment; consequently, in the case of the *Ourika* translation the translators "purposefully effaced what sometimes appeared to them as the whining undertones of the character Ourika" (ibid:16). As the introductory essay explains, the intention was to produce a text that presents "an oppressed but dignified woman of colour".

This critical intersection of women's cultures is of some interest. While the intention of the anthology is stated to be the confirmation of a tradition of women's opposition to hegemonic discourses, this tradition is not necessarily a given. It needs to be created. One way to do so is to intervene in places where images of women and women's voices no longer correspond to contemporary expectations, and make them correspond, in other words, to impose corrective measures.

Translation in an era of feminism is thus also a rewriting of former heroines, a rewriting of those gendered qualities and attitudes ascribed to women of other eras. Gender awareness has its censorious as well as its celebratory aspects.

# 3. Revising Theories and Myths

Feminist influence on translation and translation studies is most readily visible in the metatexts – the statements, theoretical writings, prefaces and footnotes that have been added to work published since the late 1970s. In these texts a noticeable trend is the developing sense of self exhibited by translators, increasingly aware that their identities as gendered rewriters enter into their work. Translators are introducing and commenting on their work, and offering explanations for it. They are exerting further influence by writing scholarly essays and 'workshop reports' that draw attention to the work of translators and the historical, literary and biographical research that often accompanies a translated text. Other theoretical work is visible in criticisms of the conventional rhetoric of translation and the myths surrounding it. This is all part of a concerted move away from the classical 'invisible' translator, the idea of the translator as some kind of transparent channel whose involvement does not affect the source or the translated texts. With gender viewed as an integral factor in textual production, attention has increasingly focused on politically aware and sometimes politically engaged translators, who are conscious of their influence on the text and may seek to impose it overtly. However, it is often considerably easier for a translator to proclaim political action in prefaces and other materials than to actually take action in the translation; this may explain the manifesto-like quality of the more combative statements, a quality that is not always reflected in the translated work. This chapter will discuss the more theoretical developments that result from the intersection of gender and translation, noting the tentative and ethically difficult processes by which women translators have extricated themselves from the classical notion of submission to the original.

## Proliferating Prefaces: The Translator's Sense of Self

Translations published in a cultural context affected by feminism are remarkable for the metatexts that draw attention to the 'translator-effect', the mark each translator, as a gendered individual, leaves on the work. In the case of translators who identify themselves as feminists, these texts display a powerful sense of the translator's identity. As Jean Delisle has shown in his discussion of the astonishing similarities between medieval translators and feminist translators, the feminist translating subject "is explicitly present, affirming feminine and feminist values"

(1993:209; my translation). In Canada, the feminist translator's sense of self is reinforced by other paratextual items such as translator/author photographs and translator/author bio-bibliographies, which in no way make a difference between the importance of the author's and translator's respective contributions or positions.

The Canadian scenario may be something of an anomaly, specific to a situation where related feminist interests have come together at the same time in a fortuitous mix. Delisle's assertion that the translator sees herself as co-author of the new (translated) work (1993:223) may not apply in all cases. The more conventional view that still pertains in many cultures has recently been described by German translator Beate Thill (1995). In a study of the prize acceptance speeches made by women translators and published in *Der Übersetzer*, the German translators' journal, Thill found that these women translators described their work in the most humble terms: they are the 'sherpa' silently bearing the burden and following in the footsteps of the master; they are 'ferrymen' (sic), transporting materials and running errands between cultures; their work is one of transition, and thus transitory. In Thill's assessment, this modesty, maintained despite impressive achievements and public recognition, is linked to problems of identity. Translators live between two cultures, and women translators live between at least three, patriarchy (public life) being the omnipresent third. Women's socialization into the private sphere, where empathy, submissiveness and industry are valued, and the double orientation they must undertake when they participate in professional life may render them uncertain, oscillating, continually having to cope with an 'ambivalence of identity'. This partially underlies their self-evaluations as 'sherpas' or 'coolies of the literary market'. Such rhetoric is what contemporary English-language approaches to translation seek to overcome, as they incorporate the subjective and gendered aspects of the 'translator-effect'.

*Asserting the Translator's Identity*

Suzanne Jill Levine goes to some lengths to explain the attraction the Cuban writers had for her despite their misogynist thrust; and her explanations clearly involve her personal identity and interests: she responds to the punning, streetwise language of Cabrera Infante because of her own New York Jewish sense of humour. She assumes the licence to 'subvert' aspects of Cabrera's and other Latin American writers' work, because she has discovered the grounds for such 'subversion' in their work. The author's own view that translation is "a more advanced stage of writing" (1983/1992:79) makes it easier for her to impose or extend wordgames or alliterations in English, since she is thereby 'advancing' their writing. The authors' literary styles favour 'subversive' multiplicity and openness leading her to draw parallels to feminist views of women as a 'subversive' element. In other words, her subjective readings of these works are the basis for her equally subjective translations. Levine explicitly includes personal, biographical information in this 'translator-effect' and draws on contemporary authoritative feminist theorists such as Domna Stanton, Julia Kristeva and Hélène Cixous who legitimate such women's work, and whose approval she considers important. These references to 'authorities' may be due to the fact that hers is an early contribution to feminist reflection on translation. But it is also because, 'in an era of feminism', she needs to justify translating (co-authoring) material that is not necessarily supportive of or supported by feminist thought.

Carol Maier's thoughts on translating Octavio Armand stem from a similar disjunction: her American feminist background conflicts with a Cuban source text that obscures or mocks women (Maier 1985). Her accompanying essay, written in the first person singular, traces her personal responses to Armand's *machismo* and tries to reconcile her feminist ethics with her role as a mediating voice of clearly patriarchal material. As in the case of Levine, the translator's own voice and feminist conscience clearly make themselves heard.

There are fewer ethical problems for translators who work on women writers and make 'lost' or new material available. They are writing within the feminist project. An interview with Sharon Bell (one of the translators of the *Translating Slavery* anthology) shows, however, that this feminist project is not always easy either. As an African-American, her sensitivity to condescending and cliched representations of blacks in texts by Germaine de Staël was much sharper than that of a European translator; Bell says, "I read [the text] according to my own suppositions, shaped in part by the racial discourse of America, and by the fact that I've personally been a victim of that discourse" (in Kadish & Massardier-Kenney 1994:175). Thus, while the other Americans and Europeans involved in the project focused on reconstituting the "tradition of women writing about race, a tradition which is a generous tradition that is not part of the racist discourse" (ibid), Bell was offended by certain text passages that repeated the type of racist discourse she had grown up with in the United States. In one instance, for example, she had to change a reference to blacks as "savages", because "[it] offended me so much I could not put down what the sentence actually said" (ibid).

This type of personal difficulty in translation has not often been the subject of scholarly discussions; in contemporary work by women translators, however, it is not unusual to find references to the translator's persona. Diane Rayor's scholarly introduction to her translations of archaic Greek women poets, *Sappho's Lyre*, clearly states

> ... the translations here reflect my individual response to the ancient poetry. My response is informed by my knowledge of Greek and of the historical context of the poetry. My gender, my background in contemporary American culture, and my personal enjoyment of contemporary American poetry also influence that response. (1991:18)

To what extent her translations reflect these personal factors is not the issue here. What is important is the woman translator's repeated reference to herself, her gender and her cultural context as influences on her work. This stands in direct contrast to the traditional view expressed in the 'sherpa' and 'coolie' metaphors and recently reiterated by Canada's most prolific woman translator, Sheila Fischman. Replying to a question about reviewers' responses to her work, she says,

> even if a reviewer says something as simple as "it reads well" [...], I'm pleased enough, because at least they are acknowledging the fact that it *is* the translator who has produced the English text. We don't ask for much more than that! (in Simon 1995:193)

Fischman doubtless belongs to an older school of translators who expect to have their work viewed as largely invisible. Feminist translators, and women working in the wake of feminist activism, reject this stand. They want recognition of the work and recognition of the translator's individuality, and are willing to move their work into the "light of accountability and responsibility" (Kolias 1990:217). Hence the proliferating prefaces, introductions and commentaries that 'flaunt' the translators' signatures (Godard 1986:7), citing biographies, political affiliations, sexual orientations and ethnic backgrounds as aspects of the 'translation-effect'. Recently Alice Parker (1993) has linked sexual practices with the attempt to develop 'multi-gendered' or 'polysexual' translation theories; De Lotbinière-Harwood (1995) has shown how personal development is intimately connected to her development as a translator; Marlatt (1989) has made her political affiliations with 'radical lesbian' thought the basis of her translational cooperation with Brossard;

Flotow (1995) has discussed the role that a translator's personal biography plays in the selection and translation of texts. As ongoing discussions in North American academic journals such as the *Publications of the Modern Language Association* (October 1996) confirm, personal aspects always affect the production of texts, translations and scholarly work. Currently, they are also the stuff of scholarly reflection. When these aspects are made apparent in translation, they undermine claims for 'invisible' aspects of translation or 'objective' readings and rewritings of any text.

## Claiming Responsibility for 'Meaning'

Not only have women translators brought their personal histories and political positions to bear on translation, foregrounding the translator's subjective input into work, they have also consciously filled the roles of scholar and teacher. This role is most evident in the essays and commentaries produced to accompany translations of works long out of print, 'forgotten' or dispersed in anthologies. It is also evident in the interpretations and explanations of the sometimes highly experimental feminist material. The translators take on the role of interpreter, educator and specialist in such literary experiments.

A good example of this approach is the work of Barbara Godard on Quebec feminist writers Nicole Brossard and France Théoret. Her translation of Brossard's *L'Amèr* (Brossard 1977/Godard 1983) is prefaced by a translator's commentary in which the interpretive thrust is already apparent. She explains certain key wordgames that could not be translated, such as the play with the silent *e* in French. She goes on to interpret the intention of these features: the *e*, she says, is dropped by the author in words like 'laboratoir' to mark the absence of the feminine in the activities carried out there. It is removed from the title *L'Amèr*, she continues, to "underline the process of articulating women's silence and moving toward a neutral grammar" (Godard 1983:7). She then indicates the methods she used to supplement her English version: graphic modes and wordplay such as that on *his*story and *her*story, which are more familiar to anglophone feminists. In a clearly educational move, she ends by drawing attention to other aspects of the text that secular, i.e. non-academic English readers might miss, noting references to contemporary French theorists Derrida and Deleuze. All this on one page. In subsequent translations – *Lovhers* (1986), *Picture theory* (1991a) and *The Tangible Word* (1991b) – the scholarly prefaces swell in size.

In *Lovhers* Godard begins with a reference to the translator's preface as a place for the translator to "immodestly flaunt her signature" (1986:7) thereby destroying the illusion of transparency, underlining the differences between two cultures and their linguistic systems, and insisting on translation as an act of reading and writing by a specific historical subject. She goes on to present *Lovhers* as the third book in a lesbian triptych in which Brossard sets up a

> sapphic semantic chain, constituting a differential analysis of what it means to write as a woman from a position of deferred meaning outside the patriarchal symbolic order ... (1986:8)

Continuing in this vein, Godard operates as literary critic, describing what to her are important aspects of the two preceding books, notably the idea that story-telling and representational detail are no longer possible, and that Brossard is in search of "a locus for the lesbian text" (ibid:9). She ends with a history of the translation of *Lovhers*, mentioning the 'ventriloquist translation' she produced when parts of it were read in public, as well as her labour over the wordplay and connotative wealth of Brossard's work. Her introductions to *Picture theory* by Brossard and *The Tangible Word* by Théoret are similar, phrased in language that curiously resembles that of her authors. Théoret, she says, is concerned with the "exploration of the construction of femininity and subjectivity, the ways in which doxa and codes inflect language, representations and bodies" (Godard 1991b:7) and Brossard transforms "holography, or writing [...] in the whiteout of the scene of production/ seduction where desire, time, memory, 'flow as information in optical fibres' [...]" (1991a:7). The fact that the translator's discourse mimics certain qualities of the authors' styles serves to emphasize the cooperation and co-authorship that Delisle (1993) has pointed out in Canadian feminist practice. It also indicates how the immediate literary interpretation of this experimental work has been frustrated by a lack of interpretive language to comment on it. The discourse is consistently interpreted in its own formulations. There is little other language for it.

While Godard's scholarly metatexts, which also include essays, book reviews and conference texts, clearly have an educational intention, brief translator's footnotes can fulfil a similar function, though not as flamboyantly. Footnoting is used extensively in the German translation of Mary Daly's *Gyn/Ecology*, where the translator explains countless references to American culture and the intricacies of the English wordplay for her German readership. Yet the translator takes the process a step further by also punctuating the body of the text with translator's notes.

For example, she is conscious of the progress anglophone feminist scholarship has made in analyzing patriarchal aspects of language, and she consistently tries to make the connection to German. When Daly analyzes the pronoun system which focuses on and reproduces the male generic, Wisselinck adds "und auch im deutschen [System]" (in the German system too; Daly 1978/1980:39) in the middle of the text. She intervenes in other places as well, providing clarification of a pronoun, presumably because Daly's text appears too vague (ibid:40), and supplying additional meanings for certain semantic items (ibid:48) by commenting on them directly in the text. Wisselinck visibly functions as an educator, assuming that her readers are not quite ready for Daly's text and need guidance.

However, this didactic approach in explaining linguistic and cultural issues in wordplay also raises problems since the translators cannot help but 'explain' via their own set of cultural values and assumptions. This can lead to curious forms of misinterpretation, with emphasis placed on semantic or cultural items the source text does not stress at all. In the case of *The Aerial Letter*, for example, the translation of Brossard's *La lettre aérienne* (1985; tr. 1988), unmarked literary resonances in the source text are identified by the translator, and the source – including title, date of publication and page number – is given in a footnote. Thus an unidentified line from Mallarmé or a borrowing from Roland Barthes in the French text is concretized into bibliographical order in the translation. The translator imposes her assessment of the value of French cultural references.

Thus, while the confrontational situations of Levine and Maier may involve a certain amount of justification in an 'era of feminism', the explanatory function assumed by some translators can reveal the limits of cultural transfer. Some material cannot be transferred; and explanations may say as much about the translators as about the text in question.

**Revising the Rhetoric of Translation**

Feminist theories have also led to a revision of the terms in which translation is discussed. This revision clearly challenges clichés such as the one promulgated by the adage *les belles infidèles*, a tag used to describe translation in 18th century France and often referred to today. It implied that if translations (and women) were faithful, they were probably ugly, and if they were beautiful, they were likely to be unfaithful. The feminist translators' sense of self and their objections to such comparisons have led to revisions of the tropes of translation.

*Tropes*

In a survey of the metaphors used to describe translation over the past centuries, Lori Chamberlain (1988/1992) explains how translational relations have regularly been expressed in terms of gender stereotypes and the power relations between the sexes. Her analysis focuses on the close link between women's oppression in language and culture and the devaluation of translation. According to Chamberlain, terms such as *les belles infidèles* express the traditional disparagement of both women and translation. Twentieth-century accounts of translators having to 'rape the text' in order to gain control of it confirm such attitudes. Chamberlain advocates a rhetoric of translation that deconstructs the power play between the sexes and between hierarchies of texts. This would ideally be a way to free our thinking from more traditional negative approaches to understanding and doing translation.

Chamberlain's argument is based on three factors. First, she demonstrates how metaphors of translation have historically been couched in terms of power relations within the family, focusing on the control of female sexuality by male authorities or male family members. Thus male translators cast themselves as 'guardians' of the purity of the text, lest it be besmirched or deflowered. They couch this guardianship in language that refers to the text as a young virgin who requires protection and moral education. The implication is that a text (and a woman) must be kept in check in order for the man/husband to be sure that the offspring – the translation or the children – are legitimately his. Second, Chamberlain shows how traditional metaphors of translation accept and promulgate violence against women; for example, when used to describe translation, the Biblical reference about the need to shave the heads and pare the nails of enslaved women before forcing them into marriage connotes an offensive abuse of power that cannot be tolerated by feminist thought. And third, Chamberlain shows how twentieth-century theorists such as George Steiner and Serge Gavronsky have exploited the language and mythology of male sexuality to describe translation in terms of ejaculation and the Oedipus complex, again both ignoring women's participation and contribution, and perpetuating a discourse of disdain or violence against them.

Chamberlain's listing and analysis of these metaphors has been highly influential for feminist approaches to translation theory; her concluding remarks, however, remain tentative. She limits herself to citing the potential usefulness of post-structuralist theories that blur the boundaries between original texts and translations, theories that look for ways to get beyond confrontational positions taken by binary patriarchal male vs feminist female viewpoints.

*Achieving Political Visibility*

In Canada, more aggressive action-oriented theories have been elabo-rated as a result of the feminist impact on translation. Godard, for instance, sees women translators usurping the source text, as well as their traditionally subservient roles in reproductive work. They 'woman-handle' the text, deriving the right to do so from the feminist source text, which sets an example of how to go about it. They display their creative role in translation in various ways, precisely in order to draw attention to the force of women's traditionally invisible work.

Godard's work has a further dimension. She attacks the more con-ventional, mainstream translations of important women's texts, focusing her critique on American-English versions of work by French theorists Luce Irigaray and Hélène Cixous (Godard 1991c:112 ff). The transla-tion of Irigaray's *Speculum de l'autre femme* (tr. Gillian Gill 1985) was published by an American university press. For Godard, the translation "use[s] the behaviour patterns and models prominent in the canonized system of the target language with the effect of turning the different into the same" (1991c:113). In other words, the translation incorporates Irigaray's source text into the dominant 'canonized' ideology which as-signs meaning without taking into account the multiple layers of feminist meaning in Irigaray's work. This produces a monosemic text – a text that strives for a single message/meaning – which may be easy to read, but, in effect, runs counter to Irigaray's intention. The translation of Cixous' work, on the other hand, produced and published in France in cooperation with Cixous, fosters and performs the feminist production of meaning by transferring the polysemic aspects of the text into an English form that is as strange as the French source text.

In this criticism of translation strategies, Godard's feminist revision of translation theories makes two major points. First, feminist post-structuralist textual theory and writing is seen to have provided women translators with the assurance that no text is neutral or universally meaningful, nor 'original', for that matter. Any text carries the mark of its producer, which is also the mark of the ideological and cultural context in which it is produced. Moreover, every reader adds their own individual meaning to the text. Feminist translators (as feminist readers and rewriters) working in a context and culture conducive to feminist writing are thus likely to produce work that is politically congruent with their time. Godard formulates this idea as follows: "Translation, in this theory of feminist discourse, is production, not reproduction" (1990:91). Elsewhere, she describes feminist translation as a 'transformance', a term she coins to

> emphasize the work of translation, the focus on the process of constructing meaning in the activity of transformation, a mode of performance ... (1990:90)

Godard thus sees translators who work in an era of feminism making their translations *perform* what the source text does in the source culture. Such theory moves the text into a third dimension, the dimension of performance. It conceptualizes translation as a three-dimensional activity that not only operates between two languages, but performs the first language *in* the second language, here bringing it to feminist life.

The interest in constructing meaning through translation confronts theories that repose on notions of equivalence. This is the second major aspect of Godard's approach. To produce 'equivalent' texts is to reduce both the source and the target texts to some acceptable, mainstream level, thus producing 'in-different' texts. Feminist work wants to disrupt acceptable, mainstream reading and writing and understanding; it wants difference. Further, it wants to draw attention to women translators' work – to the translator-effect. It is logical then for feminist translation to stress difference, deterritorialization (the fact that the text has been taken out of its territory), displacement (the exile of the text into another culture) and contamination (the confluence of source and translating languages), rather than fidelity or equivalence. Godard demonstrates this with contrastive analyses of wordplay translation; because the American translation of Irigaray avoids wordplay, it reduces Irigaray's text to one way of meaning. In contrast, the Cixous translation extends the wordplay into English, maintaining elements of the French and Portuguese of the source text. It thus responds to the multiplicity of meaning in the source text

> with a movement into the other that results in a (con)founding of languages, voices, texts. A *theory of translation as combination* is elaborated in this text in the contamination of French, Portuguese and English ... (1991c:116; my emphasis)

In this case the translation combines various languages by creating neologisms out of Portuguese, French and English, or by recognizing the various elements that make up a term and translating it in several different ways, thus stressing its foreignness. Godard here comes out in favour of "translation attentive to the letter" (1991c:118) since this opens up established, conventional meaning, and through contamination forges connections across languages and texts, as well as between women. Contamination and combination in a translated feminist text stand for women's understanding across barriers of language and culture. Further, these factors demonstrate feminists' refusal to opt for one sole meaning, and therefore emphasize multiplicity and the fact that it is sometimes impossible, even destructive, to decide one way or the other.

A strategy for translating politically 'offensive' texts has not yet been theorized. Bassnett (1992:72) writes of the impossibility of any union between a translator and an author with diametrically opposed views, while Myriam Diaz-Diocaretz (1985:19) points to the cultural differences separating women that can foreclose on any hope of mutual textual expression; the issue in this case is the problem of translating Adrienne Rich's lesbian poetry into Spanish. For the moment, such translators largely insist on their new-found right as producers of meaning to struggle with the source text, and if necessary, translate against it.

## Revising A Fundamental Myth

*Pandora's Cornucopia*

Most recently, revisions of fundamental myths of translation are beginning to emerge as gender is applied to the philosophical and mythological underpinnings of translation theory. One of these revisions criticizes theoretical preoccupations with the myth of the Tower of Babel and examines the figure of Pandora as a possible feminist alternative. According to the story of Babel, God scattered the one language that once existed into hundreds of different languages in order to punish the people for the pride and arrogance they displayed in building a tower designed to reach into heaven and thereby imitating the power of the divinity. According to Karin Littau (1995b), the continued references to this myth by contemporary theorists such as George Steiner and Jacques Derrida imply a belief in some originary language, a state of grace in which people understood one another because they spoke only one language, a pre-Babelian 'Adamic tongue'. Speculation about what happened 'after Babel' focuses on the confusion that ensued from God's intervention and tends to emphasize the subsequent communication break-down that translation never completely transcends. Citing Derrida's discussion in *Des Tours de Babel* (1985), Littau uses his elaboration of the multiple designations of Babel as not untypical of the view that language 'after Babel' is "divided, bifid, ambivalent" (1995b).

The post-Babelian discourse about translation describes translation in terms that have largely negative associations: translation is difficult, incomplete, even impossible; it is traitorous and untrustworthy. Theorists such as Derrida may take this difficulty and incompleteness as an occasion for expounding on the polysemy of language, as Littau shows in citing Derrida's phrase "plus d'une langue" and interpreting it to mean "more than one language, no more of one language" (1995b). Yet the references to Babel also suggest a certain nostalgia for a mythic time when it was not necessary to distinguish between an original and a translation.

Littau proposes another theoretical approach, via a feminist rewriting of the myth of Pandora, the other translation myth. The story traditionally relates how Pandora, the first woman of the Greek creation myth and wife to Prometheus, opened a box out of sheer curiosity and unleashed all the ills of the world, including linguistic chaos. Littau points out, however, that there are many other versions of this story. In the one she favours the box is a cornucopia that contains all the provisions to feed mankind, and connotes fertility (Littau 1995a:890). Littau argues that the many versions of the Pandora myth, collected and discussed in *Pandora's Box: The Changing Aspects of a Mythical Symbol* (Panofsky and Panofsky 1962), show that the history of Pandora "is a history of her images, which to be precise is a history of *his* images, that is, male images of her" (1995a:891). These images largely embody "phallocentric anxieties about Woman, both as regards language – the mother tongue – and as regards her gender – female sexuality" (1995b).

In rewriting the story of Pandora for use as a paradigm of translation, Littau stresses the fact that the figure of Pandora is itself a translation. It has been assigned positive or negative female attributes depending on the contexts and designs of her mythographers, her translators. In twentieth- century Freudian discourse, this figure, as a female archetype, as *Urweib*, has been associated with notions of women's 'lack' (of sex organs), with incompleteness, with silence, and with mystery. Feminist revisions of these views, notably by Luce Irigaray, conceive of 'woman's body' and 'woman's language' as a multiplicity from the outset. Thus, Pandora, with her cornucopia and her *his*story of interpretations, functions as an example of women's multiple meanings, becoming the epitome of *this sex which is not one* (Irigaray 1977). Littau revises the figure of Pandora to emphasize the richness and surplus of the cornucopia and the values feminist theory places on women's multiplicity and plurality, on the fact that 'woman' cannot be pinned down or forced into a mould. This, she says, contrasts sharply with the reductionist approach of the traditional phallocentric order that "in accordance with the procedure Irigaray calls 'hom(me)ology' focuses on *the* one (man) and views woman as '*its* other'" (1995b).

This rewriting of the Pandora myth reveals the serial nature of translation: there are always more translations, retranslations. The emphasis is thus not on the one perfect translation (that can never be achieved), nor is it on the deconstruction of the traditional hierarchy between translation and original. The emphasis is not on equivalence or on equality, nor for that matter on some mythic linguistic wholeness. Precisely because every text can be retranslated and every myth can be rewritten, seriality is a condition of translation, a condition that has no end, and no beginning. As Littau puts it,

> To translate her [Pandora's] name is therefore not finally to translate her, to translate her at last, to approximate some original condition, but rather to translate again, to retranslate. (1995b)

Littau's Pandora in translation is thus an argument for the proliferation of difference, for excess, for multiple translations as a positive, and indeed inevitable activity.

Littau demonstrates this principle in a discussion about the figure of Lulu, a figure created around the end of the nineteenth century by the German playwright Frank Wedekind. Lulu is a character of uncertain parentage: Lulu has no mother and whether Schigolch is her father, or her first lover, or both is unclear (1995a:909 fn. 12); her stage 'life' in the 'Lulu-Plays' revolves around her interaction with men — beginning as a young sex object, passing through a number of relationships, and in one version, ending in the East End of London at the hands of Jack the Ripper. Wedekind referred to Lulu as the *Urgestalt des Weibes* (the archetype of woman), yet the figure itself underwent numerous modifications in the various versions of the plays. Littau parallels the multiple versions of the Pandora myth with the multiple refractions/translations of the Lulu figure, rendered famous by her author's continuous clashes with censors and the resulting rewrites. The parallel becomes even clearer in the title of Wedekind's play: *Die Büchse der Pandora* (*Pandora's Box*; 1895/1902/1904/1988/1990), whose multiple publication dates, indicating early, censored, rewritten, re-edited and annotated versions, underscore this multiplicity. Littau demonstrates how since then "each and every re-presentation of Lulu [...] projects an image onto her by means of which her refractors [playwrights, film makers, composers, novelists, scholars] hope at last to grasp her" (1995a:901). Indeed, it is impossible to establish whether there ever was an original Lulu, and whether each 'translation' – Alban Berg's Lulu opera, G.W. Pabst's film *Pandora's Box*, or Kathy Acker's pastiche, to name just three – is even an approximation of the whole version. Attempts to reconstruct Lulu "from the hundreds of little notes that Wedekind left scattered over Europe" (1995a:902) only contribute to the ongoing series of textual productions.

Littau's analysis of Lulu's transformations ends on the same positive note as her theoretical considerations of translation: referring to the latest 'translation' of Lulu by Acker, she concludes that this work "pours lifeblood into the Lulu-figure to revive her" (1995:907). By accepting the fact of translation, by demonstrating it in the figures of Pandora and subsequently Lulu, and by thus connecting and re-evaluating the labour of translation with revised images of women, Littau places translation into a context of constant movement and change. Her work demonstrates that it is as pointless to produce theories that implicitly hark back to some original state of linguistic grace as it is presumptuous for one sex to posit itself as the measure of humanity.

Littau's work presents a view of translation as movement that she couples elegantly with contemporary feminist work in the areas of literary criticism, film criticism and psychoanalysis. Her approach demonstrates the results of a co-mingling of women's studies/feminist theory and translation studies. Having developed simultaneously over the course of the 1970s and 1980s, these disciplines have inevitably influenced each other; as Susan Bassnett has commented, feminist translation scholars "work with the idea of the in-betweenness of the translator and of the space between the poles [of the original and the translation]" (1992:66). Feminist translators are less concerned with the final product and its equivalence or fidelity than with the processes of reading, rereading, rewriting, and writing again, and with issues of cultural and ideological difference that affect these processes. Such an approach is expressed symbolically by the image of Pandora's cornucopia, overflowing with translations that bear witness to cultural and political differences.

# 4. Rereading and Rewriting Translations

Feminist initiatives of the 1970s triggered enormous interest in texts by women writers from other cultures. This led to the realization that much writing by women has never been translated at all, and to the suspicion that what has been translated has been misrepresented in 'patriarchal translation'. Thus extensive translation and re-translation activity was set off, for which willing publishers were found. As H. D. Kolias puts it in her article on the translation of the autobiography of Elizavet Moutzan-Martinengou,

> Convincing publishers about the worthiness of this work and the need for recovering it was easier than it might have been in previous decades. (1990:215)

The context created by the women's movement encouraged the development of women's publishing houses (The Women's Press in London, Éditions des femmes in Paris, Frauenoffensive in Munich, Les éditions du remue-ménage in Montreal) and the establishment of lists of women writers in translation at university as well as private publishing houses. This rush of translations has doubtless played some part in setting off translation criticism and analyses, as well as research into the work of 'forgotten' women translators.

## Reading Existing Translations

*Simone de Beauvoir*

The English translation of Simone de Beauvoir's *Le deuxième sexe* has given rise to a good example of gender-conscious translation criticism, triggered by feminist inquiry. Beauvoir's text has been referred to as the 'feminist bible', an epithet that may overstate the case but definitely points to the influence her book exerted on feminist thinking in the second half of the twentieth century. *Le deuxième sexe* was published in France in 1949 in two thick volumes; the English translation came out in 1952, prepared by American professor of zoology Howard Parshley. His version, *The Second Sex*, made the New York Times bestseller list in the spring of 1953, has seen several reprintings, and is thus considered successful.

Criticisms of the translation are primarily based on unmarked deletions of more than ten per cent of the original material. Large sections of text recounting the names and achievements of women in history have been cut from the English version; critic Margaret Simons (1983) states that the names of 78 women – politicians, military leaders, courtesans and saints, artists and poets – have thus been eliminated. The lineage of influential women, so important to feminist historiography, is thus broken through 'patriarchal translation'. Similarly, the translation deletes references to cultural taboos such as lesbian relationships, and to unwelcome realities such as the tedium of women's everyday lives. There appears to be a pattern to these cuts, perhaps motivated by the assumption that men's experiences and feelings are considered more valid or interesting than women's. Simons writes

> He [Parshley] didn't care to have discussions of women's oppression belaboured, although he was quite content to let Beauvoir go on at length about the superior advantages of man's situation and achievements ... (1983:562)

While Simons concedes that some of Beauvoir's text is longwinded and repetitive, she insists that the deletions are serious interventions in the text that should at least be marked and explained. This is all the more necessary since these deletions are the source of considerable confusion. When, for example, there are references to earlier argumentation that has been cut out of the translation, the development of Beauvoir's thought is scrambled and she comes across as a confused, incoherent thinker.

The translator, Parshley, has been somewhat vindicated in terms of his professional context: critic Yolande Patterson explains he was badgered to condense, simplify or eliminate in order to "lighten the burden for the American reader", as publisher Knopf put it (1992:43). The damage done by such edited translation may have other consequences, however. One such consequence was recently revealed through another translation, a problem that de Lotbinière-Harwood (1991:52) has discussed: when Claudine Vivier was translating Mary O'Brien's *The Politics of Reproduction* (1981) into French, she came across numerous references to Beauvoir that required back-translation into French. But O'Brien's English text cites the 'confused' English version of Beauvoir, and bases some of her virulent arguments against Beauvoir on this version. Unable to find the references in Beauvoir's original text, Vivier had the task of negotiating the misunderstandings caused by the edited *The Second Sex*. Unfortunately, Vivier does not comment on this problem in her translation *La dialectique de la réproduction* (1987).

Increasing criticism of Beauvoir's stance on sexuality and sexual practices by anglophone feminists has motivated further references to Beauvoir translations. As Barbara Klaw states, many fault her for "perpetuating patriarchal stereotypes of female sexuality" (1995:193). Yet, Beauvoir's 'clichés' may be due to censorship by her (predominantly male) translators. For example, her novel *Les mandarins* (1954) broke enough sexual taboos to be placed on the index of prohibited books by the Catholic Church in France. Its 1956 English translation 'censored' the French text in a different way, omitting scenes and changing certain passages in order "to attenuate the boldness of the sexual imagery or to strengthen the criticism of women who act upon their desires" (Klaw 1995:197). For example, the translation clearly censors the two references to oral sex, both written from the perspective of Anne, the main female protagonist. It also attenuates the language of both Anne and her adolescent daughter Nadine. In the case of Nadine's aggressively vulgar language, the English resorts to euphemisms. For instance, Nadine's bold (and unhappy) discourse on her sex life revolves around sex as a 'deal' she makes for the company of men. She says, "Comment veux-tu que j'aie des histoires avec des types si je ne baise pas" (*Les Mandarins*:350). When this is translated, "How do you expect me to have affairs with guys if I don't go to bed with them", the impact of Nadine's vulgarity (and her unhappiness) is weakened. The more accurate and more vulgar "if I don't fuck" would make the English character correspond with its French version and give better access to Beauvoir's view of her situation. The book's American editor apparently apologized to Beauvoir, stating that "in our country, one can talk about sexuality in a book, not about perversion" (cited by Klaw 1995:197). In other words, Beauvoir's *The Mandarins* was prepared for 1950s mainstream readers with 'normal' rather than 'perverse' tastes in the discourse on sexuality. Small wonder that some 1990s feminist critics find her work clichéd and patriarchal.

Feminist critics are not the only ones to discover mistranslations and misrepresentations of Beauvoir, however. In a short text published in a *French Studies Bulletin*, Terry Keefe comments on the editing and rearranging of a Beauvoir interview that was published in *Ms Magazine* in July 1972. Entitled 'The Radicalization of Simone de Beauvoir', it is a shortened version of 'La femme révoltée, propos recueillis par Alice Schwarzer' first published in *Le Nouvel Observateur* in February 1972. The fact that the entire (edited) English text was reprinted in the highly influential *New French Feminisms. An Anthology* (1980) means that this version, which "produce(s) substantive differences in the views expressed" (Keefe 1994:20) reached a wide academic public that was, moreover, not made aware of the editing.

Keefe's brief analysis of the translation and more especially of the omissions and modifications reveals that these were often concerned with "sensitive and controversial matters of feminist ideology and strategy". I cite Keefe here at some length, excluding only the page references he gives:

For instance, the exclusion of a major sequence on capitalism at the beginning of one of Beauvoir's answers undoubtedly has the effect of making her seem less anti-capitalist in the English than in the French version. Other, almost systematic, omissions result in the playing down of Beauvoir's emphasis on socialism and the class struggle, and of her insistence that she does not believe in specific feminine values ... Furthermore, the fact that the English text leaves out entirely certain striking question-and-answer sequences concerning lesbianism and women with children is bound to alter the precise impact of the interview as a whole.

Keefe is as concerned with the material that is cut from the original as he is with translation which he treats earlier. His analysis implies that feminist (capitalist?) ideology of the early 1970s probably played some role in the way this text was presented; the translation may well have been tailored for a certain white, middle-class, feminist readership of *Ms Magazine*. Keefe makes an important point when he comments that although many of the alterations "may be broadly in line with Beauvoir's thought", such a text is unfortunate in the light of the attacks on Parshley's translation of *The Second Sex* as being motivated by ideology.

## Rewriting Existing Translations

### The Bible

Gender-conscious translation criticism of the works of Simone de Beauvoir has only begun; it has not yet led to any retranslations since the translation rights are still firmly in the hands of the first publishers. The case is somewhat different for the Bible. Several sets of Biblical texts have been re-translated as a result of feminist pressure. The examples here are from two English versions, although similar work has also been done in other European languages. The English rewritings are Joann Haugerud's *The Word for Us* (1977), a translation of John and Mark, Romans and Galatians, and *An Inclusive Language Lectionary* (1983), a collection of texts from the Bible compiled as a cycle of readings for use over the church year. Both retranslations are accompanied by prefaces, footnotes and appendices, marking and explaining the translators' motivations and interventions.

The most striking aspect of these re-translations is the focus on what is termed 'inclusive language'. Earlier versions of the Bible are full of male-biased language, male imagery, and metaphors couched in such language "that people can scarcely avoid thinking of God as a male person" (Haugerud

1977:i). The effect of the "ponderous weight of masculine pronouns" (Haugerud, iii) and the metaphorical language that casts both the history of the Jews and the teachings of Christ in male terms has been to exclude women from full participation in Christian belief. Thus both translations are prefaced with remarks that emphasize the inclusive nature of Christian teachings: "All persons are equally loved, judged, and accepted by God" (*Inclusive Language Lectionary,* preface). And in *The Word for Us* Haugerud asks

> When Jesus called Peter, Andrew, James and John and invited them to become (according to the King James and other versions) 'fishers of men,' did Jesus mean that they would set out to catch male humans only? Or were women to be included? If the former, then Christianity is really for men only and women would do well to shun it. But if Jesus meant to include all people in the invitation to a new way of living, and there is ample evidence that he did, then the correct contemporary English translation of these words is 'fishers of women and men'. (1977:i)

Note that Joann Haugerud refers to the 'correct *contemporary* English translation' here, thus acknowledging and responding to the fact that the contemporary cultural context, upon which feminist thought has had some influence, determines the rereading and rewriting of such core texts as the Bible. A similar point is made by critic Paul Ellingworth, who emphasizes that the purpose of 'inclusive translation' is "to meet the needs of the intended readers" (1987:53). The intended readers might be described as people who are sympathetic to the egalitarian ideals espoused by feminist thought and are irritated by the clearly patriarchal bias of traditional Bible translations.

Feminist revisions of the Bible do not seek to change the content of the text; they are concerned with the language in which this content is expressed. Yet by revising the language, these versions change the tone and meaning of the stories considerably. The more problematic areas and proposed solutions are discussed in the introductions to both works, giving a good idea of the translators' approach to the Bible's conventionally patriarchal language. Haugerud, for example, rejects the use of words such as 'man' or 'mankind' to include women. The translators of the *Inclusive Language Lectionary* support this position, stating that "Women have been denied full humanity by a pattern of exclusion in English usage" and that "in this lectionary all readings have been recast so that no masculine word pretends to include a woman" (Introduction).

Here the verb *pretends* is surprising, since it describes 'masculine words' as deliberately fraudulent imposters and is a strong indictment of the traditional language of Bible translations.

The recasting of masculine language takes several forms: terms such as 'brethren' or 'king' which have exclusively male referents have been replaced with more specific inclusive terms such as 'sisters and brothers' or more general terms such as 'monarch' or 'ruler'. The phrases 'women and men' or words such as 'people' or 'person' replace the generic 'man', depending on the context. Similarly, the 'ponderous weight' of the masculine pronoun has been weakened; the following verse from the Revised Standard Version of John 6:35-37 gives an example of the effect of predominant masculine pronouns:

> Jesus said to them, 'I am the bread of life; *he* who comes to me shall not hunger, and *he* who believes in me shall never thirst...; and *him* who comes to me I will not cast out. (*my italics*)

Joann Haugerud translates:

> Jesus said to them, 'I am the bread of life; *anyone* who comes to me shall not hunger, and *anyone* who believes in me shall never thirst ...; and *those* who come to me I shall not throw out. (1977:14; *my italics*)

Haugerud's solution is to use neutral and plural pronouns in order to eliminate male bias. Another solution used whenever possible in both translations is to repeat a name rather than employ the masculine pronoun *he*.

A further point addressed in both translations is the language used to describe God. In the past it has been heavily masculine – 'God the Father', 'the Lord our God', the exclusive use of the pronoun 'He', and so on. In these inclusive translations no pronouns or metaphors are used which might confine God to one sex: "Gone are the lords, fathers, kings, and kingdoms" (Haugerud 1977:ii); "since God is beyond sex, just as God is beyond race or any other limiting attribute" (*Inclusive Language Lectionary,* Introduction). Instead, the *Inclusive Language Lectionary* uses phrases such as 'God the Sovereign One', or more dramatically, 'God [the Mother] and Father', where 'the Mother' is bracketed in order both to emphasize the addition, and make it optional in church communities unable to accept such innovation. The argument given in the introduction for this 'Mother and Father' translation is that the relationship which the Father/Son imagery of the New Testament seeks to describe is that "of Jesus being of the same substance as God". Thus

> if God the Son proceeded from God the Father alone this procession is both a male and a female action, a begetting *and* a birth. God is the motherly father of the child who comes forth.

The introduction goes on to cite the orthodox dogmatic tradition which "speaks boldly of God's bisexuality":

> [...] According to the Third Council of Toledo, it must be held that the Son was created, neither out of nothingness nor yet out of any substance, but that he was begotten or born out of the father's womb (*de utero Patris*), that is, out of his very essence.

The phrase 'God the Mother and Father' is thus an attempt to remove male bias from the descriptions of God and to express the belief that Jesus is the Child of God, a child that was not created, but given birth to. It is an interesting contradiction that the phrase 'the father's womb', considered a sexist elision of women's reproductive labour in contemporary Cuban poetry (Maier 1985), here serves to justify a more gender-conscious translation of Biblical texts.

In a brief manuscript text entitled "Names and Titles", Eugene Nida, famed American Bible translator and translation theorist, has commented on these types of linguistic changes. He views them as generally impracticable. In his opinion, the 'Mother and Father' translation described above would suggest a confusing reference to God and Mary for many Catholics, and even evoke a 'fertility deity'. And the repetition of the noun 'God' in order to avoid the proliferation of the masculine pronoun 'He' is not only "stylistically awkward" but "actually misleading because it may imply more than one God"(1995). He gives the feminist views relatively short shrift, ignoring the careful argumentation in the introductions to Haugerud's work and the *Inclusive Language Lectionary*. He proposes that the problems are cultural, not linguistic, and suggests two possible changes. First, he asserts, the Bible needs to be read in the context of the chauvinist male-dominated society in which it originated, and which has been perpetuated by the church. Second, church leaders must radically readjust their views about gender restrictions on church office.

The point about the chauvinist patriarchal aspects of the society in which many of the biblical texts originated is doubtless true. It is, however, also true that over the course of one thousand years of rewriting and translation by the Church, these texts have been subject to 'patriarchal' translation. The problem has thus been compounded, as scholars such as Ellingworth (1987) and Orlinsky and Bratcher (1991) confirm. Feminist translators do not seek to change historical fact, they want to overcome some of the patriarchal excesses imposed on the Bible through translation.

Nida's second point that an institution can reform itself without linguistic changes contrasts sharply with the approaches of feminist translators who posit a close link between the language used to describe God and patriarchal culture. In their view, linguistic change is an integral part of cultural change; their intention to make God an "accessible, caring, revered figure" (*Inclusive Language Lectionary*, Introduction) rather than a remote and solitary power requires changes in language before changes in church hierarchies. Indeed, they argue that the traditional terms used to refer to God have helped create certain socio-cultural realities:

> Such an authoritarian God causes earthly authorities to take their cues from 'Him'. God as Almighty Father legitimates the authority of the fathers of the church, the father of the country, the father of the family. [...] The image of God the Father has been used to support the excessive authority of earthly fathers in a patriarchal social structure. (*Inclusive Language Lectionary*, Appendix)

Here language is clearly assigned wide-ranging socio-political effects: the male-biased vocabulary used for God is seen to have an important influence on patriarchal social structures that assign authority to human males. The fact that such language also reflects the patriarchal bias of the societies that are the sources of the Biblical texts is acknowledged by these translators. Yet they view the Bible as a book that is used for contemporary religious instruction and worship, a book that must speak to "young and old, male and female, and persons of every racial, cultural and national background" (*Inclusive Language Lectionary*, Preface). The contemporary context in which "mutuality and coequality are important in the Christian church" (*Inclusive Language Lectionary*, Appendix) thus justifies these new translations. This can be seen operating in the following excerpt (from the Book of Genesis), which includes a translator's note:

> Then God the Sovereign One said, "it is not good that the human being should be alone; I will make a companion corresponding to the creature."...So God the Sovereign One caused a deep sleep to fall upon the human being, and took a rib out of the sleeping human being and closed up the place with flesh; and God the Sovereign One built

the rib which God took from the human being into woman and brought
her to the man. Then the man said,

"This at last is bone of my bones
and flesh of my flesh;
she shall be called Woman,
because she was taken out of Man."***

Therefore a man leaves his father and his mother and cleaves to his
wife, and they become one flesh. And the man and woman were both
naked, and were not ashamed.

*** This literary pun on "man" (ish) and "woman" (ishshah) intends
to show relationship rather than biological origin. The relationship is
one of equality: "bone of my bones and flesh of my flesh." (*Inclusive
Language Lectionary*, Lent 1)

This reading of the well-known creation myth amply demonstrates the effect
of inclusive language. God is no longer 'the Father', and human beings, not
'men', are being created. In the first paragraph, 'God the Sovereign One'
and 'God' appear four times; no pronoun 'He' is used to avoid repetition.
Moreover, the translator's note places the emphasis on the relationship between the sexes rather than on any essential biological qualities. The
re-translation thus deletes male bias and patriarchal authority and seeks to
establish a sense of inclusive mutuality considered more appropriate to the
context of the late twentieth century. The fact that this text may be difficult
to read says more about religious traditions and reading habits than about
the appropriateness of the translation.

## Comparing 'Pre-feminist' and 'Post-feminist' Translations

*Sappho and Louise Labé*

Feminist re-translations of parts of the Bible have attracted a certain amount
of critical attention, both within and beyond the Christian church; other rewritings of literary texts have had much less exposure to criticism. It is rare
to find studies that juxtapose and compare a number of translations of one
particular text in order to understand the ideological and contextual influences that have made the difference. Recent work by Antoine Berman (1995)
is a rare exception. The issue of gender has also motivated a number of such
studies, two of which shall serve as examples of the importance of gender
awareness in contemporary translation criticism.
    These studies take two women poets as their subjects: Sappho and Louise

Labé. Sappho, a Greek lyric poet whose work was performed to the accompaniment of a stringed instrument, lived and wrote during the 'archaic period' of Greek civilization, some time during the seventh or sixth centuries B.C. Louise Labé, the well-educated daughter of a ropemaker, lived and wrote in Lyon, France in the first half of the sixteenth century. While Sappho's work consists almost exclusively of fragments with only 700 lines remaining out of an opus of some 500 songs, Louise Labé's sonnets, published in 1555, are still widely available. Feminist interest in these poets is no coincidence; though their texts lie about 2000 years apart, both Sappho and Labé speak in strong, individual voices that clearly belong to women; they produce bold expressions of love, sexual arousal, friendship and anger, from a woman's point of view. They can thus be read as part of the lineage of women writers and poets.

Both Sappho and Labé have been repeatedly translated in the past. Contemporary studies on Sappho by Diane Rayor and Yopie Prins and on Labé by Jane Batchelor examine a number of these translations from a gender-conscious perspective, producing criticisms of the subtle, and not so subtle, differences that the numerous translations have made in the texts. While these critics do not deny that a translation must, by definition, change a text, their focus on gender issues is new in translation criticism. Diane Rayor, herself a translator of Sappho, writes:

> Most modern translations of Sappho into English have misrepresented the surviving Greek texts. The combination of the distance in time, the physical state of the manuscripts, the lack of reliable biographical information, and the poet's gender have led to the constant creation of new Sapphos by translators. (1992)

Rayor lists the poet's gender as one element that has led both to 'misrepresentations' and constant creations of new Sapphos. In so doing she seems to imply that women's texts are assigned little authority, and that in translation they have been subjected to substantial manipulation. While it is doubtful that this could ever be proven as a general truth, the studies of Sappho and Labé give good examples of 'patriarchal' corrective intervention.

Rayor's commentary focuses on the question of how to deal with the fragmentary nature of Sappho's writing. Her own English translations published in *Sappho's Lyre* (1991) reproduce the gaps as gaps, while most other available translations fill in the many blank spaces, trying to 'master' the poem or 'fix' it. Symptomatically, as Rayor shows, these repair jobs have also often rewritten the poems in patriarchal form. Thus her concern with the fragmentary nature of Sappho's work becomes a concern with gender.

One poem may serve as an example; this is Rayor's translation:

> Some say an army of horsemen, others
> say foot-soldiers, still others, a fleet,
> is the fairest thing on the dark earth:
> I say it is whatever one loves.
>
> Everyone can understand this —
> consider that Helen, far surpassing
> the beauty of mortals, leaving behind
> the best man of all,
>
> sailed away to Troy. She had no
> memory of her child or dear parents,
> since she was led astray
> [by Kypris] ...
>
> \*
>
> ... lightly
> ... reminding me of now of Anaktoria
> being gone,
>
> I would rather see her lovely step
> and the radiant sparkle of her face
> than all the war-chariots in Lydia
> and soldiers battling in shining bronze.

The narrator here compares the longing she feels for her absent friend, Anaktoria, to Helen's desire for Paris when she ran off with him to Troy. In the first stanza, the narrator claims that 'the fairest thing on earth' is whatever one loves best. The second stanza gives the example of Helen whose beauty surpassed everyone's, and who left the best man and sailed away to Troy. Since both men involved — Menelaos and Paris — are left unnamed, the clear emphasis is on Helen's desire and her resulting actions, not on the men. The third stanza informs us that Helen forgot her child and her parents because someone actively led her astray. We are not told exactly who led her astray; it could be Paris, or Helen herself, or as Rayor points out, it could be Aphrodite, whose name fits the papyrus space. The last two stanzas move from the mythological past (Helen's flight to Troy) to Sappho's present and the female narrator's feelings about Anaktoria. The fact that the last line of the third stanza and almost two lines of stanza four are missing makes the reading rather difficult. Rayor concludes the description of this poem with the following assessment:

> Sappho undertakes an important reversal in this poem. In poetry written by men in the ancient world, Helen is always the desired object, the beloved. Here, Helen and the narrator are the ones doing the desiring, the active lovers. This is a strategy in Sappho's erotic poetry: the woman is the poet and the lover, not just the object or Muse of male poetry. She is active, instead of mastered. (1992)

Rayor identifies tendencies and strategies in this fragmentary work that correspond to late twentieth-century ideas about women's agency, activity and erotic interest. Whether Rayor sees these strategies because of her own experience and context is debatable. What becomes clear, however, is that other recent, albeit more conventional translators of Sappho, including Mary Barnard (1958) and Richard Lattimore (1949/1960) did not see these strategies, or if they did, censored and ignored them. Moreover, by 'fixing' the fragmented poem, they obliterated Sappho's focus on women. Lattimore's translation is perhaps the more invasive, and reads as follows:

> Some there are who say that the fairest thing seen
> on the black earth is an array of horsemen;
> some, men marching; some would say ships; but I say
>     she whom one loves best
>
> is the loveliest. Light were the work to make this
> plain to all, since she, who surpassed in beauty
> all mortality, Helen, once forsaking
>     her lordly husband,
>
> fled away to Troy-land across the water.
> Not the thought of child nor beloved parents
> was remembered, after the Queen of Cyprus
>     won her at first sight.
>
> Since young brides have hearts that can be persuaded
> easily, light things, palpitant to passion
> as am I, remembering Anaktoria
>     who has gone from me
>
> and whose lovely walk and the shining pallor
> of her face I would rather see before my
> eyes than Lydia's chariots in all their glory
>     armored for battle.

Most notable among Lattimore's repairs to the fragment is the beginning of stanza four. In Rayor's version only the word 'lightly' exists, since as she maintains, that is "the only word actually visible in the Greek" (1992). Lattimore not only 'completes' this fragment, but he does so with material that changes the tone and the purpose of the poem. Young brides are brought into the picture, and they are fickle, excitable and irrational; Lattimore's gender bias is clear. Further, in stanza one, Lattimore changes the neutral "whatever one loves" to "she whom one loves best", making it read like a clichéd love poem. As Rayor gently points out, "this is an intrusion on the voice of the poem, perhaps a particularly masculine interpretation of female voice, in which Lattimore presumes to speak for Sappho" (1992).

Yopie Prins' work on Sappho's *Fragment 31* is an example of the possible scholarly breadth of such comparative work in translation criticism. Focusing on one 16-line poem fragment, and more particularly on the 'break in voice' in line 9, Prins analyzes translations spanning four centuries to show how Sappho's female voice, and the 'break' in this voice, have been read in translation. The 'break in voice' is also a break in the text that expresses a woman's physical inability to speak because of a rush of jealousy, and in Prins' view translates as a link between gender and lyric genre. The basis of her argument is that "through Sappho's afterlife in translation it is possible to trace the gendering of lyric as a genre simultaneously feminine and dead" (Prins, in press). Anne Carson's 1986 translation, which closely follows the word order in Greek, shall serve as a relatively literal version:

> He seems to me equal to the gods that man
> whoever he is who opposite you
> sits and listens close
> to your sweet speaking
>
> and lovely laughing – oh it
> puts the heart in my chest on wings
> for when I look at you, a moment, then no speaking
> is left in me
>
> no: tongue breaks, and thin
> fire is racing under skin
> and in eyes no sight and drumming
> fills ears
>
> and cold sweat holds me and shaking
> grips me all, greener than grass
> I am and dead – or almost
> I seem to me.

Prins' analysis of the literary interpretations and translations of this poem focus on the 'break in voice' that in Carson's version reads "no: tongue breaks". It involves a discussion of seventeenth-century aesthetic theory and Petrarchan lyric "predicated on the opposition between masculine subject and feminine object" in which Sappho is allowed to speak, "but only as a dying woman poet" (Prins, in press). It also shows how an eighteenth-century translation appropriates Sappho's poem into the dominant aesthetic, imposing upon it "the logic of the Longinian sublime" (ibid). This work by Ambrose Philips (1711) reads as follows:

> Bles't as th'Immortal Gods is he,
> The Youth who fondly sits by thee,
> And hears and sees thee all the while
> Softly speak and sweetly smile.
>
> Twas this depriv'd my Soul of Rest,
> And rais'd such Tumults in my Breast;
> For while I gaz'd, in Transport tost,
> My Breath was gone, my Voice was lost;
>
> My Bosom glow'd; the subtle Flame
> Ran quick thro' all my vital Frame;
> O'er my dim Eyes a Darkness hung;
> My Ears with hollow Murmurs rung:
>
> In dewy Damps my Limbs were chill'd;
> My Blood with gentle Horrours thrill'd;
> My feeble Pulse forgot to play;
> I fainted, sunk, and dy'd away.

Prins points out that this 'sublime' reading of Sappho enthusiastically re-enacts Sappho's rapture and even names it as sublime within the poem itself – the narrator is "in Transport tost", her "Bosom glow'd". (An interesting detail is the twentieth-century version of 'dewy damps' which reads 'cold sweat'.) Prins explains that this translation was important for Sappho reception throughout the eighteenth and nineteenth centuries, leading to "to a gradual "feminization" of the sublime" which, on the one hand, allowed women poets to imitate her texts, while on the other, it assimilated Sappho's work into a "nineteenth-century rhetoric of the sentimental suffering body" (Prins, in press). In other words, through translation carried out according to a dominant aesthetic, Sappho's name becomes synonymous with sentimental lyric. Prins argues that a more far-reaching result is that over the course of the nineteenth century, "lyric voice is gendered as feminine precisely because it does not speak" (ibid). Ironically, the 'break in voice' in *Fragment 31* which in the source text is due to an unconventional, if not taboo, love relationship – the woman's attack of jealousy occurs because a man is close to the woman she loves – is translated in such a way that it fits into, corresponds with and demonstrates women's conventional silence. Prins concludes, "Sappho survives as a text never quite sublimated into voice: a corpus used for, and ab-used by, translation" (ibid).

Prins' study is concerned with aesthetic norms and critical readings of Sappho, yet her late twentieth-century sensitivity to gender informs her analysis of Sappho's 'afterlife in translation'. Her work of translation analysis demonstrates the extent to which gender can be a productive analytical category, helping to understand the many changes that texts undergo in translation, and through history.

Since Rayor's main focus is on the problem of how to translate the fragmentary material that remains of Sappho's work, gender issues arise when the fragments are 'completed' with trivializing gendered material. In Prins' analysis, gender and the lyric genre are linked in a demonstration of how translation practice is embedded in dominant literary aesthetics. Jane Batchelor, on the other hand, approaches translations of Louise Labé asking about the effects that feminist readings of Labé have had on these works. Her strategy is to examine 'pre-feminist' and 'post-feminist' translations of the same poem as well as translators' introductions to their subject. Although she does not specifically define these terms, she implies that work done after about 1975 may be more likely to benefit from 'post-feminist' insights, and avoid crude gender stereotyping, while earlier 'pre-feminist' translations reflect a more traditional view of women. Thus traditional twentieth-century readings and translations of Labé's poetry tend "to accept a male-orientated vision of women and their writings" (Batchelor 1995), translating Labé's lyric voice as passive and submissive to male desire. 'Post-feminist' critics and translators, on the other hand, are more willing "to see Labé as potent rather than impotent, as sexually active rather than passive" (ibid).

Louise Labé's *Sonnet V: Clere Venus* is an appeal from a female speaker to Venus in which she speaks of her longing for love; it reads as follows:

> Clere Venus, qui erres par les Cieus,
>> Entens ma voix qui en pleins chantera,
>> Tant que ta face au haut du Ciel luira,
>> Son long travail et souci ennuieus.

Mon oeil veillant s'atendrira bien mieus,
    Et plus de pleurs te voyant gettera.
    Mieus mon lit mol de larmes baignera,
    De ses travaus voyant témoins tes yeus.

Donq des humains sont les lassez esprits
    De dous repos et de sommeil espris.
    J'endure mal tant que le Soleil luit;
Et quand je suis quasi toute cassée,
    Et que me suis mise en mon lit lassée,
    Crier me faut mon mal toute la nuit.

Batchelor discusses the 'pre-feminist' translations of this poem, published by Frederick Prokosch (1947) and Frances Lobb (1950) and compares them to work done by Jeanne Prine (in Wilson 1988). She finds that Prokosch's preface to his translation already sets the scene for the female stereotype he will translate into the poem. In the preface he praises Labé for her beauty and her courage, yet he faults her for her aggressive behaviour, her belligerence and the fact that "her love-life was conducted in an atmosphere of cantankerous intimacy" (cited by Batchelor 1995). In other words, he sets her up as unstable. Batchelor then shows through detailed analysis that this notion of mental instability comes across in his translation of *Sonnet V*, notably through additions that stress mental and physical decay, through the use of semantic items that connote obsessions, violations of the body, and attacks of hysteria. Similarly, Frances Lobb's translation stresses exaggerated feeling, melodramatic lament:

Bright Venus, thou who wanderest the sky
O hear my voice, which still shall cry to thee
My heavy travail and long misery
As long as in the heavens thou shinest high.

More tender shall I find my wakeful eye,
My stubborn tears will learn to flow more free,
More clement will my nightly vigil be,
As long as thou art witness to my cry.

Now is the time when tired eyelids close
And gentle sleep brings peace to heart and head.
But oh, the whole day long my sorrow grows

> And when, at last, when almost rent
> In two with grief, I seek my hateful bed,
> The whole night long my sorrow I lament

Through the prominent use of the second person pronoun "thou who wanderest", "cry to thee", "thou shinest high", Lobb creates a sense of the speaker's dependence that is nowhere to be found in the source text.

Jeanne Prine's 'post-feminist' translation, on the other hand, strikes a different note from the very beginning. The speaker demands that Venus hear her voice. There is an emphasis on the relation between the speaker and Venus - "on the dilemma of unrequited love that links these two women" (Batchelor 1995). Through the use of more active verbs Prine underlines the speaker's strength and her awareness that she must live through this sorrow. Prine's version reads:

> Bright Venus, who wanders through the sky,
> Hear my voice that rich in pain shall sing,
> To you as long as you appear to shine,
> Above, of love's long strain and tired care.
>
> My watchful eye will be more moved,
> And seeing you more tears will shed;
> The tears will bathe my soft bed better,
> With your eyes bearing witness to my pain.
>
> Now human spirits grow fatigued,
> And by sweet rest and sleep are seized.
> But I bear pain while daylight shines:
>
> And when I am completely broken,
> Arranged exhausted on my bed,
> I must cry out my agony all night long.

Batchelor's comments on Lobb's and Prine's renditions of the last stanza are particularly insightful. In Lobb's version, she notes the 'hyperbolic drama' in the line 'rent/ In two with grief' which heightens the melodramatic effect. She comments on the addition of the word 'hateful' to bed which changes *"mon lit*, the place for sleep but also the place for the sexual act" into an expression of the speaker's misery. Similarly, she remarks on an important reversal in the last line: in Labé's version the emphasis is on the speaker having to cry out her pain, since this is placed in the first part of the line,

"Crier me faut mon mal". In Lobb's translation, "the whole night long my sorrow I lament", the duration of the agony is emphasized, not only by the word order but by the term 'lament', which connotes a less resolvable condition than the source-text *mal* (pain) from which the speaker can presumably recover. Prine's 1988 translation, on the other hand, translates this last line to point out the importance of the task of suffering: "I must cry out my agony all night long". The use of the verb of obligation parallels Labé's *faut* and shows the speaker drawing strength from her agony instead of being an "emotional wreck, the victim of what others, what the goddess has imposed upon her" (1995). Further, Batchelor asserts that Prine's translation "Arranged exhausted on my bed" acknowledges and expresses the speaker's lucid self-awareness: she is writing her suffering for a readership, self-consciously fashioning her experiences into a poem that presents her "arranged on [her] bed", "glorious even in defeat".

The type of comparative analysis of translations that both Batchelor and Prins develop requires painstaking labour as line-by-line comparisons have to be made. It also demands acute sensitivity for minute changes in literary tone and message, since the arguments hinge on word associations, word order, and subtle changes in rhythm. Finally, a good understanding of the socio-cultural contexts and aesthetic norms prevalent in the periods in which the works were written and the translations were produced helps explain the impact that social movements, cultural politics and literary fashions may have on these texts. In these and other examples of translation criticism, it is clear that the women's movement has not only affected translation practice, it has also had an influence on critics and scholars involved with translation.

## Recovering 'Lost' Women Translators

Resurgent interest in women's writing has led to discoveries of and further research on women translators; and since in many historical periods women were restricted to translation a considerable number of 'lost' women translators have been uncovered. An excellent example of this type of work is *Silent but for the Word* (Hannay 1985), a collection of essays on Tudor women as patrons, translators, and writers of religious works. Margaret Hannay's introduction to the volume clearly describes women's situation in sixteenth-century England. Citing numerous conduct books that admonish women to be silent, and describing the education system that kept women uninformed and voiceless, Hannay shows how religious texts offered the rare educated and intellectual women the only escape from this restrictive situation:

> ... women were permitted to break the rule of silence only to dem-
> onstrate their religious devotion by using their wealth to encourage
> religious education and publication by men, by translating the re-
> ligious works of other (usually male) writers, and, more rarely, by
> writing their own devotional meditations. (1985:4)

Hannay claims that the restriction to religious writing had two results. First, the wealth, energy and learning of a substantial number of noblewomen was channelled into the production of numerous religious works, from which the emerging Protestant church clearly sought to benefit. Second, these same wealthy, energetic and learned women on occasion subverted the texts they were working with, using the medium of translation to "insert personal and political statements" which they were otherwise prevented from making (1985:4). In other words, translation afforded these silenced women an in-tellectual occupation into which they occasionally, and perhaps never deliberately, allowed something of their own voice to enter.

### *'Subversive Activity' in the English Renaissance*

The anthology presents 'lost' women translators, among them historical figures as well known as Queen Elizabeth I of England, as women with subversive clout. It examines their personal and political interventions in texts and explores the religious and political contexts which both hindered and 'permitted' learned women to participate in public letters. The control exerted over educated women by the authorities in charge of public discourse and the way women translators subverted this control through their translation is the thread running through much of the copious English-language research on Renaissance women translators.

   Like *Translating Slavery* (Kadish and Massardier-Kenney 1994), the anthology *Silent But For The Word* is compiled from the perspective of feminist historical research and the search for a lineage of energetic and effective women. It presents a number of Tudor women as transla-tors – Margaret More Roper, Elizabeth I, the Cooke sisters and Mary Sidney – as well as other women as poets and patrons and writers of religious material. In the discussions of the translations, the emphasis is often placed on the moments where these women's own voices become audible. In an era when women's work was highly restricted, personal moments in their translations are seen to reflect their own experiences and understanding of contemporary sociopolitical situations.

   The clearest example is that of Elizabeth I. Anne Lake Prescott (1985) analyzes Elizabeth I's translation of Marguerite de Navarre's *Le miroir de l'âme pécheresse*. She makes the claim that Elizabeth's traumatic family history enters into her translation. The 'slips', errors and omissions visible in the otherwise largely literal translation by eleven-year-old Elizabeth may reflect her confusions about her situation (1985:68ff). Living in the household of her stepmother Catherine Parr, Henry VIII's sixth wife, Elizabeth had experienced the executions of her mother Anne Boleyn and her stepmother Catherine Howard. She had witnessed the divorce of Anne of Cleves and the death of Jane Seymour. Prescott shows that her translation of this French poem that expresses religious perceptions in terms of family love and relationships reveals a deep ambiguity, if not anger, toward the father figure. To give just one example from Prescott's reading:

> No mere mortal husband, says Marguerite, will pardon an adulterous wife; rather, there are plenty who from revenge have had them judged and put to death: "Assez en est, qui pour venger leur tort,/ Par les juges les on faict mettre à mort" (ll.587-88). Elizabeth wrote, "There be inoughe of them, wiche for to avenge their wronge, did cause the judges to condemne hym to dye." (1985:70)

Prescott notes that *hym* (the husband?) is crossed out and replaced by *them*. Does this refer unconsciously to Elizabeth's family situation and reveal her rejecting the power she has seen wielded by her father? One can only speculate, applying the theories and findings of twentieth-century psychoanalysis. Prescott shows that such questions are not inappropriate here, since issues of gender confusion and authority persist in the translation, perhaps fuelled by Elizabeth's difficulties with what Prescott describes as the poem's "passionate evocation of God as a great king and judge who is kind to daughters and does not execute adulterous wives" (ibid:71). In this case, the translator's personal history as one of a number of obviously vulnerable women is an important factor affecting her work.

Similar awareness of political vulnerability is seen in the translations of the Cooke sisters, whose published work is limited to religious texts. The critic Mary Ellen Lamb also explores their use of translation in private correspondence. In their letters they use translation to make confidential or private information inaccessible to spies, and to make veiled threats that might appear too direct in English. Further, their facility with a number of languages is proof of the erudition they were forced to suppress in public. Thus, while it is impossible to claim a subversive impact for their published work, Lamb makes the claim that though politically vulnerable, these Renaissance women were forceful and resolute, and able to deal competently with their society (Lamb 1985:124). Mary Sidney's translations are also presented from the perspective of a politically endangered aristocratic clan. Beth Wynne Fisken (1985) examines her translations and paraphrases of the *Psalms* to show how they reflect her ideas, tastes and experiences. In particular, Fisken focuses on the extent to which Sidney's experiences as a wife, mother and female member of an endangered family find expression in the metaphors and images she uses, leaving traces of the otherwise silenced female voices of Tudor England.

This anthology and Tina Krontiris' book *Oppositional Voices: Women as Writers and Translators of Literature in the English Renaissance* (1992) clearly spring from the motivation to establish a history of resistant women. This desire lends energy to the research and motivates the patient, time-consuming analyses of the translations. Women translators are seen as 'subversives' by reason of the simple fact that they dared to publish work in an essentially hostile environment. And they are particularly 'subversive' when they address the issue of gender, regardless in how circumspect a manner, because in doing so they display their awareness that the limitations under which they work are imposed upon them rather than inherent in them.

A number of middle-class translators of the period show interest in gender by rewriting the conventions of male rhetoric in feminized form. In "Theorizing Translation in a Woman's Voice", Douglas Robinson (1995) explores the texts about translation that were written by Margaret Tyler, Katherine Philips, Suzanne du Vegerre and Aphra Behn. He views their feminized use of the discourses of courtly love, patronage and morality as a sign of subversive activity. Margaret Tyler, for example, takes the traditional claim by male writers that women are their (silent) muses or their patrons and uses it to claim the right for women to express themselves as translators or writers. Her argument is roughly that women should be allowed to read and translate what men dedicate to them, and moreover, there is no difference between a man dedicating a story to a woman and a woman writing her own story. While this last assertion is not entirely logical, Tyler's transfiguration of the silent and passive female muse/patron into an active reader/translator/writer is a notable departure from the conventional rhetoric of patronage.

Similarly, Katherine Philips's self-deprecating commentary on her translations seems to be a parody of the rhetoric of courtly love normally used by socially inferior men trying to glean interest or funds from an aristocratic lady patron. Philips presents herself as a translator who must be 'courted' before she will translate. Her work, she says, is so 'poor', she needs to be begged to do more of it. She describes her relationship with a patron as follows:

> ... and the next time I saw him, [he] so earnestly importuned me to
> pursue that translation that to avoid the shame of seeing him who
> had so lately commanded a kingdom become a petitioner to me for
> such a trifle, I obeyed him so far as to finish the act in which that
> scene is ... (cited by Robinson 1995:163)

Her pretence about the trifling quality of her work scarcely conceals the fact that she has the upper hand as she gives in to torrid requests for more of her translations. Philips thus uses the rhetoric of courtly love but applies it to the figure usually placed in a lower position in the social hierarchy.

Robinson also shows how a translator exploits the moralist position traditionally held by men to impose her own taste in writing. Writing at the time of a burgeoning middle-class that stressed the values of hard work, stability and minimal ornamentation, Suzanne du Vegerre trims the texts she translates of all excessive stylistic and descriptive materials. She explains this with what Robinson calls 'a maternal voice', censoring what she feels is inappropriate for her readers' moral condition.

In these examples then, women translators of Renaissance England are shown to wield a certain power, despite the restrictions imposed upon their activities. Some seem to wield this power self-consciously, aware of their interventions and their appropriation of conventional jargon. It is this apparent awareness that makes their work attractive to researchers working on gender issues.

*Nineteenth-Century Women Translators*

North American commentators such as Robinson and Hannay may be relatively quick to assign subversive value to the Renaissance women translators they discuss, eager to find traces of individual voices and experiences in their work. Susanne Stark, writing on English women translators in the nineteenth century, takes a more sceptical position. Hers is largely a labour of identifying and listing translators, and reporting on the positions they assume in their prefaces and other metatexts. She thus presents the names and dates of a number of more or less well-known women translators, among them Marian Evans (George Eliot). And while she also acknowledges the effects of dominant discourses which made translation a "specifically female flight from public recognition" (1993:37), she categorically rejects one particular concept that has fuelled much feminist theorizing of the twentieth century: Virginia Woolf's idea of the 'Angel in the House'. Woolf describes this 'Angel' as a product of nineteenth-century gender conditioning, as a 'familiar species of woman in the last days of Queen Victoria who was "intensely sympathetic", "immensely charming", and "utterly unself-ish" (Woolf, cited by Stark 1993:33), and whose "purity and grace threatened her [Woolf's] very existence as a writer" (Stark 1993:33). In Stark's view, this 'Angel' in fact had little hold over the nineteenth-century translators she unearths; they travelled, learnt foreign languages, negotiated contracts and developed entrepreneurial skills. In other words, Stark argues that women translators such as Marian Evans or Sarah Austin were perfectly able to produce important work despite nineteenth-century social practices.

Stark thus avoids asking the psychological questions that the scholars assembled in Hannay's anthology pose, and she refuses to speculate on the effects the translators' social positions might have had on the translations. Eliot's doubts about how her male author would react to his work being translated by a "young lady ... that most contemptible specimen of the human being" is noted by Stark (ibid:36), but not developed on a psychological level. Nor does Stark see much psychological hindrance in Sarah Austin's wish to "hide behind inverted commas" (ibid:40) in order not to upset patriarchal role models. Basing her study of these women's achievements on the statements they make and on occasional comments by male contemporaries, rather than on the translations they produced, Stark concludes that nineteenth-century England saw its fair share of influential women translators, who were oblivious to the 'Angel in the house' that so hampered Woolf and subsequently came to stand for women's roles of passive submission and support for men in the Victorian period.

Stark's work is valuable for the way it unearths the work of many women translators; her moderate critical position presents an interesting contrast to the more politically engaged and more emotional North American work.

One further study of a nineteenth-century woman translator deserves mention here. The American Margaret Fuller published translations from German in the early part of her career as a writer, publisher and member of New England writers circles. Her translated works include *Tasso*, a translation of Goethe's *Torquato Tasso*, completed around 1833 and published posthumously in 1860. These translations have been largely overlooked, eclipsed in importance by other work that Fuller went on to produce. Christina Zwarg (1990), however, focuses on Fuller's translation work, arguing that "through translation Fuller found a way to begin a 'translation' of women into democratic culture" (ibid:464).

Fuller's *Tasso* is discussed in the context of her interests in pedagogy, in literary influence and in ideas about an 'interpreting community' based on dialogue and discussion. Zwarg also surveys Fuller's relationships with Emerson and other New England intellectuals, her interest in the education of women as well as the decisions she made regarding the publication of reviews, excerpts of translations, critical essays and full translations. Some of these decisions reflect the tensions between gender, power and authority that drive the drama, *Torquato Tasso*, and pertain in Fuller's own world. For example, Zwarg suggests that Fuller sees parallels between her own intellectual environment, in particular in her relationship with Emerson, and the complex relations between the characters of the play, where issues of gender, education, social conditioning and interpretation are at the root of the dramatic tension. Locating Fuller in the role of the rare nineteenth-century American woman educated in the classical and European languages, Zwarg suggests that Fuller's translation highlights the female figures in Goethe's drama, "fram[ing] the drama in such a way that it actively releases the radical if supplementary potential of women" (1990:473).

Fuller's translation is shown to operate in a number of different ways; for example, it intensifies the misogynist rhetoric that Tasso indulges in at the end of the play, thus erasing the difference in the way he perceives the two female characters. Although the differences between the two women have been an important theme since a large part of the play revolves around their relationship, Fuller intervenes in such a way that Tasso, in his disappointment and humiliation, treats them both as 'sirens'. In Act IV, Tasso's commentary on one of the women, reads: "Leonora Sanvitale, / Die zarte Freundin! Ha, dich kenn' ich nun!". Fuller translates: "Leonora Sanvitale - the soft siren./ I know her now" (Cited in Zwarg 1990:488). The sarcastic reference to the 'zarte Freundin' (literally tender/gentle (woman) friend) takes on a more aggressive tone in 'soft siren'. When Tasso also calls the Princess 'a siren' at the end of the play, he echoes this first reference, reducing both women to the same, and emphasizing the "circling of desire and pain" (ibid:472).

Fuller's translation also heightens the restrictive gender codifications within which Tasso and the Princess move and think. For example, it employs such "explosive terms" (Zwarg 1990:480) as 'captive' and 'slave' where Goethe's original uses neither. When the Princess is thinking about the influence of Tasso's poetry, she says to him in German:

> Und soll ich dir noch einen Vorzug sagen,
> Den unvermerkt sich dieses Lied erschleicht?
> Es lockt uns nach, und nach, wir hören zu,
> Wir hören, und wir glauben zu verstehen,
> Was wir verstehen, das können wir nicht tadeln,
> Und so gewinnt uns dieses Lied zuletzt.

This passage occurs at a point where the Princess has confided in Tasso, the poet, her dissatisfaction with her suitors and her dependence on him and his poetry in her loneliness. Fuller reads this type of seduction according to the hierarchies of power and control (Zwarg 1990:480) and translates:

> Thy poem's highest praise
> Is that it leads us on, and on; we listen,
> We think we understand, – nor can we blame
> That which we understand, – and thus become thy captives.

The use of the word 'captive' by the Princess is not necessitated by the German source text, which says 'the song wins us over'. The effect of the term is heightened in Tasso's impassioned and passionate response when he uses the word 'slave'; in German he says: "Ja, fordre was du willst, ich bin dein!" (Ask whatever you will, I am yours), while in Fuller's translation his response reads: "Whate'er/ Thou wilt, ask of thy slave". Given the resonances that the terms 'slave' and 'captive' had for an American audience, where "white women were the primary subjects in captivity narratives while black men were central to abolitionist tracts about slavery" (ibid), these semantic choices considerably increase the tension and the issues of power obtaining between the two characters. In comparison, the Princess' text in a translation published by John Prudhoe in 1979 is rather mild:

> It has another secret of its own.
> Your song entices us to hear its tale
> Of love. We listen and we understand
> And what we understand we cannot blame.
> And so, at last, you see your poem wins us.

This version eschews questions of power and authority. Instead, it emphasizes the love theme, by specifically using the term 'love' and by creating the enjambment that places it at the beginning of line 3. Yet, the 'love' that Tasso's poetry may kindle in the Princess (and which she does not name outright in German), and the 'love' he desires, are two different phenomena, ruled by their power relations.

Perhaps the most interesting aspect of Fuller's translation of *Tasso* is the role it played in her intellectual environment. This was enhanced by her giving the play the simple title *Tasso* rather than *Torquato Tasso*, which had the effect of distancing the play from the actual historical character and connecting Fuller more closely with the work. As the text touched on so many relevant themes discussed among the Concord circle where it circulated in manuscript form, "Tasso", the name, became for Fuller and her friends, particularly Emerson, "the signal of their own complicated interaction"

(Zwarg 1990:473), as is evidenced by Emerson's references to the play throughout his essays.

As in the case of the recuperation of Tudor women translators, Zwarg emphasizes Fuller's 'resistant' translation, claiming that Fuller's relationship to language assumes a

> subversive content, a subversion simultaneously influenced by her education and the "translation" of her gender in America afforded by that education. (ibid:464)

Zwarg links personal aspects of Fuller's life and social context to the selection of work she translates, to the portions she publishes, to the changes she makes in the texts and to the prefaces and commentaries she writes. Zwarg not only presents another 'lost' woman translator, but invests her with subversive force. As someone who is aware of her exceptional situation as an educated woman, Fuller recognizes the need for a 'female frame' in which to translate and publish. She thus published excerpts of her translation together with an article on Bettina von Arnim's *Günderode*, another German work that featured the intellectual relationship between two women. Zwarg implies that by multiplying and interconnecting the nurturing intellectual bonds between women through her choice and juxtaposition of texts and her comments on them, Fuller used translation as a vehicle for expanding and developing the space of women's resistance to those structures in 'democratic' America that had made her own classical education an exceptional gift.

*La Malinche*

A very different recovery of a woman translator occurs in the feminist re-evaluation of the Mexican figure of *La Malinche*, also known as *Dona Marina* or simply *Malinche*. Biographers (Cypess 1991) describe her as a woman of Aztec origin who was sold into slavery as a child, and later became the interpreter and wife/mistress of Cortes in sixteenth-century Mexico. Her translations do not exist on paper, of course, yet eyewitness accounts express admiration for her remarkable linguistic and mediating talents and her character. A feminist revision of this figure has been set off by the "damning cultural judgements that label her a whore, the mother of a race of *mestizos*, and a traitress to her country" (Mirandé and Enríquez 1979:24). In conventional myths and stories, Malinche is considered responsible for causing the downfall of Mexico through her services as an interpreter, a responsibility that has resulted in the term *malinchismo* being used in Mexico today to denote selling out to foreigners. But she has also come to symbolize the humiliation of conquest, particularly sexual conquest. She is held responsible for being the mother of a bastard race, a woman who consorted sexually and politically with the conquistador.

Mirandé and Enríquez' feminist rewriting of this translator figure approaches the issue from a psychological perspective. It presents the historical details of Malinche's life and tries to understand her options and her motives "in light of her circumstances as a trade object, a trade commodity who passed from one set of hands to another" (1979:29). By this account, her position as a mediator is due to the fact that she had been sold into slavery and had lived in several Indian societies. This multiculturalism is what allows her to function as a neutral, mediating party in a conquest that would have taken place in any case. Another position (Del Castillo 1977) stresses the religious and political aspects of Malinche's work with the Spaniards. She had experienced Aztec suppression of the Mayas and other tribes in the name of Aztec superiority and by the terrorist means of mass slaughter for religious purposes. This may have persuaded her that Cortes represented the lesser evil. An early convert to Christianity, she thus helped bring about the collapse of a reign of terror.

Whatever the explanations, feminist rewritings of the story of Malinche dismiss the ominous parallel between the 'treacherous' sexually active woman and her role as the 'traitorous' translator. Instead, feminist rewritings focus on her historical realities, her social position and her motivations, seeing her as a gifted linguist and strategist, a mediator who sought to avert bloodshed, and an unfairly maligned cultural scapegoat.

The work currently being done to locate and rehabilitate 'lost' women translators and to reread their lives, their translations and other writings has most certainly been inspired by the late twentieth-century interest in gender. It stems from the need to recognize the contributions that women have made to society in spite of enormous obstacles; it seeks to revamp and re-establish a lineage of intellectual women who, by dint of their persistence against substantial odds, managed to have an influence on their societies. The research is made more urgent by the fact that translation has historically been described in gendered terms, closely and negatively associated with women. As Margaret Hannay (1985:9) points out, translation in Tudor England was considered 'defective', enabling John Florio to declare that "all translations are 'reputed femalls'" and thereby apologize for his *own* labour in this degraded activity.

Hannay picks up on the major issues that gender-conscious critics and researchers often raise in translation studies: women have been deliberately excluded or discouraged from prestigious forms of education and hence from participation in the public sphere; they have thus turned to translation as a 'humble' option. And since translation has traditionally been coded as a secondary, reproductive and even 'traitorous' activity, associated with misogynist stereotypes of women, their work as silent, passive, transparent interpreters who do not threaten the male establishment, has at times been tolerated. Historical views of women and the political controls imposed upon them thus find an easy parallel in the similarly 'degraded' position of translation. It is not surprising that feminism has something to add to translation studies.

# 5. Criticisms

The criticisms that have been addressed to feminist approaches to translation and translation studies can be divided into two general types: those that reflect positions outside feminism and favour an 'objective' approach to scholarship and writing, and those that come from within the widening boundaries of feminism and support the view that gender makes a critical difference. The criticisms uttered within a feminist ethics are of particular interest since they advance the discussion, raising new issues, adding diversity, and generally rendering feminist work on translation more complex. They challenge positions, foster debate within feminism and engage with other less politically-motivated analytical and practical work on translation.

## Criticism from Outside Feminisms

Despite a substantial body of work on gender as a category that affects human experience, and therefore human knowledge, scholarly work based on notions of 'universality' or 'objectivity' is still being produced. This type of scholarship is in itself a form of criticism of feminist or 'inclusive' work since it both ignores contemporary developments and hampers their reception. Especially in those cultures where the women's movement has developed less influence than in the Anglo-American academic sphere, this type of critical response has a number of negative consequences. In such an academic climate, interest in gender can be labelled as unscholarly and threaten a career to the extent that feminist work ceases to be produced. Or, work that addresses gender issues may not be published or disseminated, and thus not trigger discussion, controversy or new ideas. Scholars who continue to work in this area may be marginalized and rendered uncertain, a handicap in the formulation and presentation of innovative insights.

Such responses to gender-conscious scholarship may justify themselves on the grounds that gender issues are too emotional, too partisan, too ideological, in fact, too subjective for real scholarship. Yet this view harks back to notions of objectivity, which as feminist work has not tired of showing, do not even exist within feminisms, and may at most apply to the basic human needs of communication, food and shelter.

A more serious response to feminist initiatives in Bible translation is developed in a short text by Eugene Nida (1995), which raises the issue of 'gender neutrality'. According to this view, work that highlights socio-cultural or political inequalities and ascribes them to gender difference seeks to achieve gender neutrality. Since, however, most living creatures, the argument goes, are of either female or male sex, "there are no cognitive models to form a basis for understanding such gender neutrality" (Nida 1995). Biological sexual difference is thus seen to make gender a given that must be recognized and expressed in language, and that cannot be linguistically transgressed. Social change can be made solely on the sociopolitical level, with each society or group adjusting its cultural practices to remedy an untenable situation.

This argument is directed against language reform, one of the foundations of feminist activity. In this case, Nida argues that 'inclusive' language in Bible translations is "no really valid solution to the issue of gender neutrality" (ibid), claiming that only radical change *within* the group (here, the Christian church) will lead to changes in the inequitable roles assigned to women and men in the church. Yet this begs the question about how isolated or complacent and conservative groups find out about other ways of being or seeing if they do not have access to new language. How do such groups even come to realize that when a term such as 'Father' is used to denote the powerful spiritual benevolence assigned to the Christian god this is a reflection of its own patriarchal bias, and further strengthens it.

Moreover, it is doubtful whether feminist work actually seeks to establish gender neutrality. This seems to be more of an argumentative move 'from outside feminism' than a feminist goal. A rather flippant response might take the term *androgyny* as an example: it presently refers to the union of the physical characteristics of both sexes in one being, a union that could be taken as a form of gender neutrality. However, the fact that 'andro' (the 'male' part of the word) comes first should raise serious doubts about the 'neutral' aspects of the word and the condition.

Another type of criticism levelled against gender-conscious translation addresses the various kinds of metatexts that accompany translations of experimental work and the numerous anthologies of women's writing. These are seen as superfluous 'noise' that distracts from the actual text. Such criticisms presumably support the view that a text must be able to stand on its own; if it cannot, there is something flawed or weak about it. While it is doubtless true that some texts can stand on their own in translation, this is often due to the fact that a long history of interpretation, rewriting and scholarly interest has created a tradition for that text. Since this has not generally been the case with women's writing, and even less so with new experimental writing, metatexts may well serve a translation, providing the foreign material with a way into the translating culture and making it accessible to the readers.

A case in point is the two-volume anthology *Women Writing in India* (Tharu and Lalita 1991/1993) published by The Feminist Press of the City University of New York. One of its many aims is to make the writing of very diverse women from the different ethnic and religious groups living in India available in English – both for readers in India who don't know some of the other languages and for an international English-language public. The anthology presents writing by women from 600 B.C. to the late twentieth century. In such an undertaking, the metatexts are invaluable; they contextualize material that is foreign to the many anglophone readers who, as Gayatri Spivak (1992:189) has suggested, are culturally blinkered due to the wholesale disregard of anything that does not stem from Graeco-Roman antiquity. Further, the metatexts offer insights into the selections made, discuss the authors whose work was considered untranslatable because "standard forms of English [are] (too) sanitized to stretch into anything that resembled the scope of [this writer's] idiom" (Tharu and Lalita 1991/1993, Preface, Volume I, xxii) and situate Indian women's work comparatively within the shifting contexts of international women's work. The anthology would be considerably weakened without the metatextual apparatus, which mediates these translated texts in order to make up for the lack of a tradition of reading them.

## Criticism from Within Feminisms

### Elitist Experiments

Experimental feminist writing has not escaped charges of elitism since its first appearance in the early 1970s. It has been easy to see that this writing was not meant for popular consumption but was aimed at an educated readership with some knowledge of the burgeoning women's movement and the willingness to engage in linguistic work. The claims made by some of its authors and proponents about the 'avant-garde' nature of this material further alienated some of the willing readers for several reasons. For one, the artistic avant-garde has been associated with the efforts of more or less decadent young men whose groups excluded or silenced women as effectively as most other groups. Second, work that is labelled avant-garde is seldom seen to have an immediate or concrete socio-political effect, functioning instead in the realm of art and aesthetics, even avoiding the political arena. Many feminists, however, wanted to institute visible and rapid changes in their societies, and experimental writing did not seem a very direct way of doing so. Third, the interest that 'avant-garde' experimental writing garnered in the academic sphere caused the devaluation or exclusion of other types of writing by women. This problematic has been discussed at some length, by Rita Felski among others. Felski comments on some of the radicalizing claims made in regard to French feminist experiments:

> It is impossible to make a convincing case for the claim that there is anything inherently feminine or feminist in experimental writing as such; if one examines *l'écriture féminine*, for example, the only gender-specific elements exist on the level of content, as in metaphors of the female body. (1989:5)

Felski goes on to dismiss arguments that experiments in form can be described as specifically feminist and to claim that French feminism overestimates the political effects of language games. Moreover, she asserts, the focus on experimental work "limits oppositional culture to the reading and writing experiments of an intellectual elite" (1989:6). She argues in support of writing that reflects the experiences, histories, and biographies of women in different parts of the world, in different racial and class groups and at different historical periods. This writing is as important as experimental work since it reflects and promotes feminism as the social movement it is, and moves it into a more popular public sphere.

The opposition that Felski sets up between French feminist experiments and more socio-critical types of expression can certainly be transferred to the translation of experimental work. In translation, the problem is compounded by the fact that when experimental texts are translated they not only move into other languages but also other cultures, which can make them appear even more exotic and elitist. A recent article by Canadian Robyn Gillam (1995) is one of the first to level charges of elitism and cultural inappropriateness, even meaninglessness, against English translations of texts by Nicole Brossard. Thus far these translations have generally been read in silent awe at Brossard's intellectual achievements and the virtuosic linguistic manipulation of the translator, in an atmosphere that evinced uncritical admiration of this challenging literary material.

Gillam's major point is that certain translations make the already difficult source material even more obscure. They produce versions that seek to extend already complex wordplay into the English text by privileging sound associations over meaning. Moreover, in order to create these sound effects in English, the translator has deliberately mistranslated. Gillam suggests that these translations can only be addressed to a small coterie of academics who are already bilingual and can marvel at the linguistic accomplishments of both author and translator.

These charges are based on a major point of cultural difference. English and French-speaking Canadians have inherently different political relationships to their respective languages. For Quebeckers, language has been and continues to be a political issue of daily life while this is not the case for most English-speaking Canadians. Thus, Brossard's deconstructive language games mean something different in a text in Quebec than they do in the rest of Canada. Because they derive from and respond to a different linguistic history, they have a different political value. And when Brossard experiments with the gendered aspects of French, thus taking Quebec's concern with language one political step further, she takes it well beyond the threshold of most English-speaking Canadians. Finally, since this focus on language has little in common with forms of political activism in English-Canadian culture, feminists are "at a loss to translate either [Brossard's] texts or her ideas into their own culture" (Gillam 1995:12). This is why, Gillam suggests, Godard's translations focus on the sound of the words rather than their sense, and why the translations of French feminisms and *écriture québécoise* are "reduced to an intellectual game where there exists nothing but words and their meanings" (ibid:11). A similar criticism of such translation was uttered in 1985 by Evelyne Voldeng. In a review of the English version of Brossard's *L'Amèr, ou le chapitre effrité* she attacks the translation for "creating a puzzling ambiguity that only a bilingual reader understands when referring to the source text" (1985:139). The translation is more difficult and more confusing than Brossard's original work, and patently aimed at readers who are already bilingual. Why translate, one might ask.

This 'elitist' type of translation thus presupposes that readers have an academic background, a bilingual and bicultural understanding of the text as well as an appreciation of linguistic change as a political catalyst. Luckily, it is one of a number of feminist approaches, which, in their totality, may balance each other out.

*Opportunist Feminist Bandwagon*

'Opportunism', 'hypocrisy' and 'theoretical incoherence' are terms that Brazilian critic Rosemary Arrojo (1994, 1995) has applied to feminist activism and interventionism in translation. These are harsh words which Arrojo bases on the statements translators and academics have published in essays and translation prefaces. Arrojo does not discuss actual translations. Instead, she comments on the context feminists "are so bravely fighting to construct" and on their "much deserved space within the prevailing, phallogocentric world of men" (1994:159), phrases that express a distinct distance to the political activism and agency of the Anglo-American women's movement. It is thus hard to say whether Arrojo works 'from within feminism'; doubtless, issues of cultural difference between Brazilian and Anglo-American feminisms underlie her criticism, though they are not stated.

Arrojo bases her attack on three major points: it is opportunistic to claim to be faithful to the tenor of a text, as Suzanne Levine does, and yet admit to deliberately intervening in the translation for feminist reasons. In Arrojo's eyes, Levine, as well as Lori Chamberlain, who supports her practice, are merely exploiting the context feminist theory and praxis have created; they are trying to make their own politics count. She says it is contradictory to claim 'fidelity' to a text one deliberately 'subverts'.

This complex issue is reminiscent of the problem with Brossard translations discussed above. Translators such as Levine and Godard work with source texts whose deconstructive and experimental moves make them appear to be wide open for interpretation. The source texts 'explode' meaning, they multiply meanings and do not offer any 'therapeutic', easy-reading forms of literature. They lend themselves to equally multiple interpretations by the translator, which Godard honours by doubling and tripling certain words and Levine exploits to undermine grossly narcissistic *machismo*. The translators thus see themselves operating in a close relationship with a text that is itself a 'subversive' entity, which, in turn, licenses their creativity.

A second target of Arrojo's criticism is the feminist 'double standard', the tendency to describe as violent and aggressive the theories produced by George Steiner or the comments made by John Florio, while refusing to see that feminist intervention in texts is no less aggressive. She cites the use of the term 'hijacking', which critic David Homel applied negatively to Lotbinière-Harwood's interventionist work on Lise Gauvin's *Lettres d'une autre*. The term was recuperated by commentators (Flotow 1991) and translators such as Godard to describe the process by which a feminist translator applies 'corrective measures' to the work in hand, appropriating the text in order to construct feminist meaning. The term graphically expresses and acknowledges the struggle for the control of meaning, as it was played out at a particular moment in Canadian literary politics. Its ironic recuperation in this context escapes Arrojo.

Arrojo's third point is the 'theoretical incoherence' she sees in feminist discourses on translation. This, she says, is located not only in claims about 'subversive fidelity', but is evident in the general references to post-structuralism and deconstructionist work upon which feminist critics and translators base some of their ideas. Explaining that according to Derrida "no meaning can ever be 'reproduced' or 'recovered' but is always already created, or recreated, anew" (1994:158), Arrojo asserts it is theoretically incoherent for feminist writers/translators to claim to "recreate meaning, anew". This orthodox Derridean view thus cancels out women's optimistic assumption that they can act upon a text, independently. For Arrojo, the forceful, interventionist, creative approaches that have come to define feminist work in translation are a mere mirage; there can be no agency.

Arrojo thus implies that feminist theory is not part of recent deconstructive theory. Some would claim the opposite, demonstrating the extent to which their work has deconstructed long-held views about universal truths and objectivity as well as political and cultural structures and myths. Further, Arrojo appears to support the deterministic position that since meaning is always being reconstructed anyway, ideas about being able to intentionally re-create meaning are nothing but self-delusion. This is a position that is diametrically opposed to ideas about language as a vehicle for social change; it also ignores the fact that feminists have consistently selected theories or bits of theory they find useful to apply to their particular projects. This tactical application of theory may be incoherent for some, for others it is strategic.

### 'Being Democratic with Minorities'

Perhaps the most scathing critique of certain types of feminist work in translation comes from Gayatri Spivak. Of Bengali origin, she is a literary theorist and practising translator who has published commentaries on western (English and French) translations of third world writing. While she focuses on the translations of women's writing, she claims that her work could apply quite generally to most texts translated from third world into western languages. In 'The Politics of Translation', Spivak formulates extensive criticism of the 'with-it translationese' used for third world literature and the ideology that makes possible such careless, homogenizing work that "literature by a woman in Palestine [..]

resembles, in the feel of its prose, something by a man in Taiwan" (1992:180). This essay takes up and expands on earlier work in which Spivak asserts that there is a "ravenous hunger for third world literary texts (by women) in English translation" (1988:253). This hunger has been triggered by benevolent liberal feminist interests as well as by the vague desire to remedy racial bias within western feminism. She implies that this benevolent interest may, however, do more to serve Anglo-American purposes and careers than it does to propagate understanding of the situations in which many third world women live, and only few write. The situation is made worse by the fact that Anglo-American feminists seem to want to read third world literature as documentary and realistic depictions of life, while the "literatures of the First World have graduated into language games" (1988:267). These two approaches – the 'benevolent' will to understand and disseminate third world women's cultures and literatures, and the naive view of third world literature as realism – heavily influence the translations and misrepresent the works and cultures they claim to speak for.

Spivak criticizes what she calls the "old colonial attitude [that] is at work in the translation racket" (1992:187). Translations are done to comply with the publisher's convenience, with classroom convenience (accessibility/readability), and with the "time convenience for people who do not have the time to learn" (1992:185). Among these people she places translators who have boned up on third world languages in order to respond to a vogue of interest but who know little about the history of the language, the history of the author or about what she calls 'language-in-and-as-translation'. Arguing that literary writing never simply imparts information, Spivak stresses the rhetoricity of language. This is the particular style of the source text that carries considerable meaning within its own cultural and literary context and in relation to it, as well as in relation to western forms of expression. It is what makes any text specific to its author and its cultural context and time, but also reveals individual resistances to the traditions it springs from. When convenient or benevolent translations are made, or when the translator "cannot engage with, or cares insufficiently for, the rhetoricity of the original" (1992: 179), then a "neo-colonialist construction of the non-western scene is afoot" (ibid:179). In other words, the following situation exists: easy-reading translations of third world materials are produced; the source texts are selected by relatively uninformed academics who cannot or do not distinguish between resistant and conformist work, often labouring under the false assumption that anything by women writers will do; this creates a situation in which 'democratic' western consciences may be salved, but where, in fact, western laws of force apply. In effect, these translations construct a third world as well as a third world literature that correspond to western tastes. They provide a facile way of being 'democratic with minorities'.

Spivak backs up this criticism with contrastive examples from her own translations and those of others as well as with western interpretations of Indian religious myths and songs. She explains that painstaking labour and research are necessary for a translator to become intimately familiar with third world source languages and their cultural histories, in order to then identify and respect the rhetoricity of their writings. This preparation is more necessary than for a translator dealing with European languages, since these languages have garnered most of the powerful western academic interest, and in-depth knowledge about their histories and literary traditions is available. But Spivak also warns against assuming that someone like herself, who has a third world background but a western education, would necessarily do a good job. The effects of colonialism, that can cause such a person to exoticize or denigrate third world literary production, might also preclude the kind of translation she wants. Finally, she criticizes any easy assumption about women's solidarity, the basis for the 'benevolent' approach. Such solidarity is impossible if only because of the differences between languages which cause women to experience reality in different ways. While the idea that women have something in common is often useful and may make contacts between women easier, it is akin to ideas about 'universality' that have been debunked by feminism and other post-structuralist theories.

Simplistic notions about women's solidarity were debunked well before Spivak wrote these articles, for example, when women of colour began to make themselves heard against white middle-class feminism. However, Spivak's application of the notion to translation, and particularly to the 'with-it translationese' that some women's texts are subjected to, is pertinent. It undermines the assumption that privileged western feminists can ever claim to truly 'give voice to' or otherwise represent the women they deem oppressed in third world societies.

## Revealing Women's Cultural and Political Diversity

Much of the criticism of gender-awareness in translation that comes from within the feminist camp draws attention to the cultural differences between women. Feminist thinkers have long acknowledged these differences, and there are few who would want to describe any experiences or ways of being as 'essential' to all women. However, the factor of gender, the effect of 'learning to be a woman' is felt in every society, even though it will mean something different in every society, and probably in the subgroupings within any one society. The attendant differences of political affiliation, ethnic background, religious beliefs, racial and economic difference are important enough to make understanding or solidarity between women on the grounds of gender alone relatively unlikely. This 'truth' has been repeatedly demonstrated by translation. On the other hand, however, translation has also opened paths for women to find new ways to see and deal with their particular situations. It has also allowed gender-conscious women to communicate and at least seek to understand something of the other women's culture. A certain progress in the translational and transcultural relations between western women may perhaps be visible in the following examples.

In 1970s North America, translation led to an awareness of the cultural differences that can hamper feminist interaction between even the most willing partners. When the writings of French feminists, such as Hélène Cixous, began to appear in translation, the discomfort that anglophones felt at the inherent foreignness of the material led to significant resistance. Doubtless more attention had been paid to the 'rhetoricity' of *these* texts than to that of third world women's writing, since anglophone critics did not report easy-reading experiences. Instead, they felt troubled and excluded by this 'extraordinarily glamorous' discourse (Gilbert 1981:7). The interpretive gap between American and French women academics reading and writing at the same historical moment was made visible precisely because of translation. Critical or interpretive work would not have revealed this gap as drastically; indeed, such metatexts were called upon to mediate the translations. Women thus became aware of the great cultural and political differences that lie between supposedly related Western societies, and began to revise what theories they may have had about solidarity and understanding. Thus, while on the one hand feminist theories have posited *gender* as a unifying principle that binds all women into a common experience of oppression, the experience of translation has revealed the great diversities of culture and politics that separate women from each other. This is visible in any number of areas touched upon as a result of translation: for example, in certain German translations of American women's writing, we find unwitting perpetuations of preconceptions about American 'lack of culture' (Flotow, in press); in the Anglo-Canadian/ Quebec situation, the issue of differences in language politics arises as a major factor (Gillam 1995, Scott 1989); in multi-ethnic societies, the ethnic differences felt even by second and third generation immigrants affect translations (Flotow 1995). And as the editors of *Women Writing in India* confirm, the translation of women's writing in such multi-ethnic societies poses further problems of authority and dominance of one group over the other (Tharu and Lalita 1991/1993).

On the other hand, however, the copious translation of women's writing and publications on gender whether in North America or Europe, or in hefty anthologies of texts from the third world, make evident the importance of gender in cultural and scholarly life. This vogue of translation also makes available new ways of thinking and operating. Translation gives access to other women's lives as well as to the linguistic processes they adopt to influence power structures in their particular contexts. It may therefore trigger new ways of living, thinking and taking influence in the target contexts. Women's difference, revealed in translation, is thus implemented "as a crucial strength" (Lorde 1981:100).

Such gendered influence through translation has rarely been discussed in European publications. One exception is a recent 'workshop report' in the German publication *Der Übersetzer*, the journal of the German association of translators. Karen Nölle-Fischer (1995), a translator of contemporary English fiction asks "Können weibliche Schreibweisen Bewegung in die Geschlechterbeziehungen bringen?" (Can women's writing styles bring about changes in gender relations?). Nölle-Fischer wonders about the effect that English women's writing in German translation might have on German readers. She sets about answering this question from the experiences she has gathered as a translator, and she does so in order to evoke the connections between writing, reading and experience.

Translation has shown her the immense benefits of a language in which gender need not be immediately revealed in the nouns, adjectives or participles an author uses. In English, she points out, it is possible to write an entire love poem using words such as *friend* or *lover* and never tell whether the lovers are heterosexual or homosexual. It is also easy to postpone revealing the sex of a protagonist, thus heightening the effect of gender when this mysterious person turns out, say, to be a woman. It is thus possible to maintain ambiguities, leave things up to the readers' wishes or imagination, and not impose one particular reading. Since this ambiguity is very difficult to maintain in German or other gender-marked languages, it is therefore also 'unthinkable', that is if we agree that to a large extent the language we think in influences what we *can* think. Nölle-Fischer implies that in German it is therefore harder to undermine conventions about sexual relations or imagine alternatives.

Translation, however, reveals this different way of thinking and intimates it as a possibility.

Nölle-Fischer explores linguistically innovative presentations of gender-relations in works by Doris Lessing, Annie Dillard and Alice Munro. These differ substantially from what is available in contemporary German women's fiction, which has experienced a slacking-off after the heyday of feminist creativity of the 1970s. For her, translation offers new vistas to readers, or at least provides them with enough of an irritant to encourage them to widen their horizons and move beyond the conventional knowledge propagated by their own language and its political and cultural structures. Translation offers an opening into a new language, a view of the different ways of being that this language makes possible. But this also requires some effort from the reader (1995:8):

> Die Aufforderung an die Leserin lautet, die sie in Anspruch nehmenden Fragen weiterzuwälzen, eine Irritation in das reibungslose Ineinander des immer wieder gleichen Denkens hereinzulassen, die sich in Gedankenfolgen verhakt und für neue Wendungen und Fügungen sorgt.

> The challenge for the (woman) reader is to further develop the questions that interest her and to disrupt the smooth continuation of endlessly same thinking. This will tangle thought sequences and ensure new expressions and constructions. (My translation)

It is debatable whether this 1995 challenge to German readers represents an advance on the anxious responses that American academics had to linguistically experimental women's writing in 1981. However, these two situations demonstrate the extent to which differences between women and their cultural backgrounds intersect in translation. Criticisms of elitism, political opportunism and hypocrisy or colonialist 'translationese' discussed above stem from these differences. They render the questions raised by translation more complex; they demonstrate the diversity of gender issues and, perhaps unwittingly, function as part of a survival strategy. Where there is no controversy or discussion, there is often only silence.

# 6. Future Perspectives

Recent work in cultural studies is introducing issues of gender into the discussions on colonialism (McClintock 1995), on orientalism (Lewis 1996) and examining them in the light of constantly changing political affiliations (Funk & Mueller 1993). Gender thus remains fertile ground for research in the human sciences. New avenues of thought have been opened by the development of gay and lesbian studies and theoretical works that question the basic duality of gender. At the same time, contemporary explorations of cultural difference which effectively undermine any claim for the universal applicability of findings about gender can only lead to more productive and creative work.

The perspectives for the study of gender and translation are tied to these developments and the plethora of possibilities they offer. Nonetheless, academic work is also affected by such constraints as funding, cultural acceptability of the topic and consensus on what constitutes academic research. Research perspectives may thus be restricted by dominant cultural assumptions, by academic priorities or power structures that determine what counts as scholarship in a certain place at a certain time. Given a relatively open-minded academic setting, however, research perspectives in the area of gender and translation are multiple, precisely because the field is quite unexplored. The following is a brief listing of such perspectives and a series of questions that may serve to prompt scholarly undertakings.

## Broad Historical Perspectives

In translation studies it has been more customary to formulate prescriptive theoretical models than to study existing translations. The study of translations, especially translations of lengthy prose fiction, involves the juxtaposition of source and target texts, their comparison and the painstaking analysis of findings presented in the context of the changing relations between the cultures involved. As Ria Vanderauwera (1985:5-15) points out, such studies have been eschewed, not only because they require detailed examinations of long and complex texts as well as in-depth knowledge of the two cultures and their historical contexts, but also because the study of translations has not been considered as prestigious as the study of 'national literatures' or the production of more abstract theory. However, the work done by researchers such as Margaret Hannay and Tina Krontiris, Yopi Prins and Jane Batchelor shows that the study of women's work as translators and in translation can offer important new perspectives. Since so little of this type of comparatist work has so far been published, much remains to be done.

In regard to historical perspectives on gender and translation, the following questions might be considered:

• *What roles have women played as translators?* Contemporary critics tend to posit gender as an important fact in a person's life and work. How has gender affected the work of translators in the past? Have they resisted or undermined the dominant norms and orthodoxies of the societies they lived in, and if so, how did they do this? Does their work provide any non-canonical views of the cultural 'truths' and assumptions propagated by dominant cultural systems? How and why has their work survived over time, and what has been its influence?

One might, for instance, consider the gender effect in Marie Bonaparte's French translations of Freud and enquire about the influence it had on the early reception of Freud in France. Similar studies of the translations of Thomas Mann by Lowe-Porter would doubtless yield interesting results. On a different note, the translations produced by numerous twentieth-century women writers – Marina Tsvetaeva, Marguerite Yourcenar, Monique Wittig – could be examined for the links between their twofold creative pursuits. While twentieth-century work may be most accessible, such analyses could be extended to any historical moment, and any geographical or cultural region.

• *How have women fared in translation?* Have works by women writers been accorded different treatment from those of men? Can any difference be posited as a general maxim, or must it remain restricted to individual writers? Has translated literature by women had a different history than similar work by men? Were there moments when women's writing in translation made significant breakthroughs (the nineteenth-century novel, perhaps)? In which cultures did this occur, why and what were the effects? A delicate question, so far motivated by anecdotal information, might address the alleged improvement that translations of prize-winning women authors undergo. Toni Morrison's work in French and German translation is said to have undergone substantial change after she was awarded the Nobel Prize. Has this in fact been the case? And what are the characteristics of a 'better' translation? How do such changes affect the reception of the writer's work?

## Contemporary Perspectives

Contemporary perspectives on gender and women's writing have raised issues about the effect of feminist activism on the creation and reception of texts.

- *The feminist politicization of translators and translation*: Have translators in general become more gender-conscious and how does this affect their work? To what extent have different cultural contexts limited or promoted gender-awareness in translation? How do politicized translators deal with parts of texts they find problematic or offensive? How does gender-conscious translation affect the selection of texts to be translated and the reception of translated texts? How does the situation differ from culture to culture? And how are individual cultures involved differently? For example, one might ask what effect the heavy influx of Anglo-American texts dealing with gender politics has had on German writing and scholarship. Similarly, one might trace the eastward movement of gender-conscious materials after 1989 as translation and reception increase in former East Bloc countries and are affected by changes in economic and political conditions.

- *The technical aspects of feminist writing and translating*: Since much experimental feminist writing pursues similar goals such as the subversion of patriarchal language and the creation of a utopian new literature, there are many technical challenges in the translation of this work. What strategies are employed to translate experimental discourses? How are neologisms, wordplay, deconstructed metaphors and proverbs translated? Are there global strategies that may be applied to several different language pairs? To what extent are paratexts useful, necessary, or superfluous 'noise'?

- *Reception and market research*: How are feminist textual politics transferred to other cultures that are reluctant to accept change or are hostile to such cultural politics? Are differences made according to genre? Is children's literature handled differently from adult literature? Does the treatment of popular writing in translation differ from that of 'high' literature? How do gender issues affect other translated media such as film, television series, news reporting, interviews with political and other personalities? A broader research topic might also approach the question of marketing: To what extent has public and scholarly interest in gender issues created a market for translations, and for what kinds of texts? Given a certain number of canonical writers in Western feminisms, which culture translates which texts, and why? For example, what are the dynamics that make work by certain French writers readily available to North American scholars while others remain untranslated (Penrod 1993)?

- *Cultural difference*: As the work by Gayatri Spivak and Robyn Gillam has shown, all translation is faced with negotiating cultural difference. And since feminism means something different in every culture, the issue is heightened in texts where gender is foregrounded. In the wake of international women's conferences where women from every part of the world struggle to reach consensus on issues rendered sensitive precisely because of cultural, ethnic and religious differences, it is clear that translation is an important factor both in facilitating and in hindering understanding. The study of translations can help untangle cultural differences between women, locating them below the surfaces of texts, analyzing and understanding the political and social contexts that produce such differences.

## Public language policies

Public language planning is a factor in numerous countries. Whether through advisory systems or through outright regulation, numerous countries have taken the lobbying of feminist pressure groups into account and established policies regarding gender and language. Since all public language policy also affects translation, the following questions might lead to avenues of research:

- To what extent do government language policies and language planning programmes take gender issues into consideration? How does this affect translation in bilingual or multilingual countries?

- How far do government surveys, opinion polls, census documents reflect gender awareness, especially in bilingual or multilingual societies? Are such documents prepared in a dominant language and then translated, and if so, how are gender issues dealt with? Further questions along these lines might address private sector language policies as business ventures become increasingly international and multinational and need to address women and men equally. How do translated handbooks – medical, technical, travel, popular science materials – reflect, or deflect, gender bias? To what extent do gender issues enter into the translation of pragmatic texts?

*Interpreting*

Interpreters are often aware that gender affects their work, especially in cases where a woman interpreter works in an area of discourse dominated by men – military matters, international politics, high finance. Yet few researchers have explored the field. When questions on gender and interpretation are raised, they often take the form of anecdotes that circulate around issues of the following type:

- Do male and female voices have a different aural authority? To what extent and under which conditions does this authority affect an interpreter's credibility?

- Does gender difference affect the ability to switch codes? Does women's 'oral culture' – their supposedly innate bilingualism – aid in acquiring and honing interpreting skills?

- To what extent are gender issues involved when interpreting moves out of the field of the international conference into the community and areas such as refugee hearings, law courts, hospitals?

- What kind of political resistance can/do interpreters offer when having to deal with political issues such as gender, environment, medical research or political asylum? Has gender politics changed women interpreters' views of their roles, perhaps rendering them more politicized language transfer professionals?

There is little doubt that in a global situation where intercultural activities involving language transfer are both required and enhanced by modern communication and transportation systems, research perspectives in many aspects of translation studies are promising. When gender is factored in, the situation becomes more complex. It also becomes more political. On the academic front, gender issues have historically been ignored and are only now beginning to be recognized due to the pressure the women's movement has been able to exert in some academic settings. In the area of cultural difference and its translation, gender definitions also raise political questions about the respect shown toward cultural specificities and the tendencies of some translating cultures to adjust culture-specific aspects to their own socio-political views. Given that gender affects every individual who reads and writes or is otherwise engaged in language transfer, it offers fertile ground for further research.

# 7. Concluding Remarks

The intersection of feminist work on gender and translation studies comes at a time when the field of cultural studies is the focus of much academic interest. Yet work in cultural studies tends to reserve the concept of translation for metaphorical use to describe the increasingly global aspects of cultural production and the situation of those who are exiled, displaced or otherwise caught between different worlds and different languages. As Sherry Simon points out, it is not uncommon to talk about women "'translat[ing] themselves' into the language of patriarchy, migrants striv[ing] to 'translate' their past into the present" (Simon 1996:134) Yet the material realities of translation are occluded in such metaphorical use. This is all the more true when scholarship is conducted primarily in English or on texts translated into English and the 'translation effect' of those texts is not recognized as a feature of their meaning. The erasure of translation that occurs when women are viewed as 'translating themselves into language' rather than *translating* recalls certain theoretical discourses in the realm of translation. Theories that concern themselves with overarching abstractions about 'translatability', 'equivalence in difference' or 'dynamic equivalence' and view translation as a primarily linguistic operation carried out between two languages eschew the concrete issues of cultural difference, of context and of the discursive possibilities and options available at a specific historical moment. When, however, the focus is directed toward the cultural and historical specificities of translation – as it is when gender is brought into play – attention is drawn toward the way meaning can be and *is* constructed in translation. The recognition of the *gendered construction of meaning* in any textual practice makes possible a more differentiated understanding of translation processes. Not that gender is the only element in cultural difference that translators, readers, researchers, theorists, or people interested in *Kulturpolitik* need to be aware of; there are numerous others. However, the demonstration of the importance of gender coupled with the demonstration of the 'translation effect' in feminist translation draw attention to the subtle shading of cultural difference.

By its presence alone, feminist work in translation practice, theory and criticism undermines the temptation to formulate generally applicable theoretical models. It asserts and explores difference, not only in terms of gender attributes and limitations, but also in the ways such differences function and are expressed in language. Further, by revealing how the practical work of translation must come to terms with the enormous differences *between* women, feminist translation studies makes it difficult to emphasize sameness, or assert some essential qualities in women or in translation. When, for example, the contemporary translators of eighteenth-century abolitionist texts admit having to 'tamper' with these texts on various different levels in order to make them conform to today's requirements, they are demonstrating the kind of influence that every form of rewriting – translation, criticism, anthologizing, reviewing, editing, film adaptation – exerts on a text. 'Meaning' is a feature of a specific time, constructed for a specific purpose, by a specific individual working within a specific context. Because feminist translation practice and criticism clearly demonstrates this, it encourages us to ask the following questions in other, less overt translation situations "who rewrites, why, under what circumstances, for which audience?" (Lefevere 1992:7).

Like feminist translation practices, Lefevere's questions point to the partisan nature of rewriting, and specifically translation. He emphasizes this position by claiming that "rewritings are produced in the service, or under the constraints, of certain ideological and/or poetological currents" (1992:5); he goes on to assert, however, that "such currents do not deem it to their advantage to draw attention to themselves as 'merely one current among others'" (ibid). This raises another point regarding feminist work on gender and translation: this particular 'ideological current' *does* deem it important to draw attention to itself. It 'flaunts' its achievements, exhibiting the kind of revolutionary fervour that seeks to attract converts unafraid to publicize and promote their affiliations. There is only little of the surreptitious influence-taking traditionally associated with translation. Instead, translators and translation critics working within an ethics of feminist thought tend to assume personal responsibility for their texts, unwilling to disclaim their part in text production or to 'hide behind the inverted commas' of translation like Sarah Austin did in nineteenth-century England. On the contrary, such 'woman-identified' translators and critics (Maier and Massardier-Kenney 1996) largely declare their responsibility and positionality toward the text and the community it is destined for.

This responsible positioning is vital since it avoids gross generalizations on the one hand, and the dissemination of culturally and politically questionable material about women, or feminisms, on the other. Instead, it allows the negotiation of difficult ideological and cultural rifts between women. In translation studies, it makes possible a more differentiated negotiation of similar rifts between texts, cultures, and other human affiliations. Three factors make up this attitude: 'identity politics', 'positionality' and 'the historical dimension' (Alcoff 1994), all of which are demonstrated in contemporary juxtapositions of gender and translation, and all of which I deem important for translation.

Identity politics in translation and translation criticism involve acknowledging the translator's personal interests and needs, and viewing this individual as someone with specific cultural and political characteristics that will determine their insights, opinions and work on the text. These characteristics may affect the choice of text, the response to the text, the translator's view of her or his function in the communicative situation. Spivak's writing serves as an example of such an approach: she writes in the first person singular, describing how her critical work as well as her translation practice is affected by conversations, by other translation experiences from French and Bengali, by her experience of Western feminisms and 'Indian' women's issues as well as by the Indian caste system and American academia. All of these factors play into her work; they serve to situate it in a certain context.

'Positionality' further relativizes this personal aspect of the translator's work by making identity

> relative to a constantly shifting context, to a situation that includes a network of elements involving others, the objective conditions, cultural and political institutions and ideologies, and so on. (Alcoff 1994:116)

This concept allows translators and critics to acknowledge and account for constantly shifting personal and intellectual settings and the effects of such shifts on scholarly 'knowledge' and on textual production. In translation, it is clear that the 'era of feminism' has made many more projects possible than in earlier generations. It has helped create a number of institutional conditions that complement the feminist identity politics of individual translators (and perhaps hinder those not so identified). The prevalence of women's publishing houses and the interest of general publishers in women's writing has allowed translators such as de Lotbinière-Harwood to choose to work only on texts by women. In contrast, the effects of the 'political correctness' reaction or 'backlash' as well as changing economic conditions will doubtless have a somewhat more deleterious effect on feminist productivity. Finally, the concept of 'positionality' can also shed light on the Anglo-American bias in work on gender and translation; conversely, it can aid in understanding why it may be difficult to produce such work outside the English-speaking community.

The third aspect, the historical dimension, articulates a concept of gendered (or other) subjectivity "without pinning it down one way or the other for all time" (Alcoff 1994:114), construing it instead "in relation to concrete habits, practices and discourses, while at the same time recognizing the fluidity of these" (ibid:115). This factor makes it possible to accommodate numerous different, even oppositional and highly critical approaches within the feminist purview; these differences are due to 'historical dimensions', examined and worked through in response to other discourses. The debate over 'elitist' translation and the earlier discussions about the elitist nature of experimental writing exemplify this dimension, demonstrating the effects of generational and cultural differences within one and the same project. Similarly, the recuperation of Tudor women translators into the fold of Anglo-American 'subversion' reflects this historical dimension, showing how textual 'meaning' and 'meaningfulness' are constantly being re-evaluated.

The issue of constant re-evaluation raises the last point I wish to make in these concluding remarks: the conjuncture of feminist gender studies and translation reveals the extent to which translation gives clues about the 'hotspots' of cultural exchange. Or to put it in Christina Zwarg's terms: "translation has increasingly become the vehicle through which history, meaning and language come to crisis" (1990:463). Through the critical and informed analysis of translations, through the critique of translations along the lines of the work done by Yopie Prins on English Sappho translations (in press), or by Antoine Berman on the French translations of John Donne (1995), our awareness of the many types of cultural difference becomes acute. Moreover, we realize to what extent the gaps between cultures differ at different historical moments. The conventional view of translation as a grandiose humanist bridging of differences can thus be reviewed to acknowledge the fact that translation is about difference. And it often accentuates difference. The work of 'women-identified' or feminist scholars and translators amply demonstrates this reality.

# GLOSSARY

*canonical texts*: texts considered part of the heritage of a particular community and thus a mandatory part of the school/university curricula. Feminists (and other marginalized groups) have challenged the canon and demanded that 'marginal' literatures, reflecting the work of less powerful groups in society, also be studied.

*construct*: the term is used in conjunction with 'cultural', 'gender' or 'social' to emphasize the constructedness of political and social conditions. Viewing gender as a 'cultural construct' would imply that gender is not a natural condition but a condition that humans are taught to fulfil or live up to.

*deconstruct*: to dismantle, or take apart; in contemporary literary criticism the terms 'deconstruct', and in particular, 'deconstruction', refer to applications of contemporary French philosophical thought – especially work derived from philosopher Jacques Derrida –, that undermines and takes apart concepts hitherto considered unquestionable facts.

*empowerment*: a neologism developed in the theories and discourses of feminist and other marginalized groups. It refers to the self-confidence and 'feeling of power' that can be acquired through critical thinking and group solidarity.

*'era of feminism'*: the term is used here to refer to the last thirty years of feminist activity, and to the productive and supportive (for women) atmosphere created by this activity.

*feminism(s)*: the theoretical and political aspect/element of the 'women's movement' which seeks to improve the lot of women in society. Feminism is a historically recurring phenomenon, though the interpretation of women's public activities will vary according to the context in which they are studied. Contemporary Anglo-American feminist historians tend to interpret the development of women's groups in the church of the late Middle Ages – the Beguines – as a movement with feminist motivations. On a secular level, the works of Christine de Pizan in the late Middle Ages are viewed as feminist writing. Similarly, the 'Précieuses' can be seen as a seventeenth-century form of feminism, while eighteenth- and nineteenth-century social activists and public figures who called for women's legal rights and suffrage are clearly forerunners of twentieth-century feminisms. 'Second-wave' feminism generally refers to the activism that began in the 1960s and has had enormous influence on the late twentieth century. The plural form – 'feminisms' – is used today to recognize the many different types of political thought and activism incorporated in this term.

*gender*: the term is used to designate the socio-cultural attitudes that go with biological sex. Such attitudes and behaviours are acquired as girls and boys grow up. They vary according to the historical moment, the place, the ethnic group, religious beliefs, and social class the child is born into. Originally focused on male and female gender, the term is now being blurred to incorporate other sexual orientations.

*gender affiliations*: this refers to the choices adults may make about the gender they wish to identify with.

*gender awareness*: this term refers to a person's consciousness about gender, their realization that gender plays a role in human interaction and productivity.

*gender hierarchies*: this refers to the importance and power a society allots to a certain gender. Feminist thinkers assert that the patriarchal systems of most contemporary societies assign decision-making qualities, a public voice, and political power primarily to men.

*gender issues*: any questions, problems or discussions raised with regard to gender in society.

*gender politics*: the recognition of the political nature of gender relations and the subsequent attempts to influence these relations through overt or covert political means such as affirmative action.

*gender studies*: academic studies concerned with issues of gender – in history, in political science, in business, in medicine, and so on.

*machismo*: exaggerated or clichéd masculinity, often maintained at the expense of women.

*misogyny*: disdain or hatred for women.

*Pandora's box*: the myth of Pandora has been cited as one of the "two main conjectures" in mythology that are used to explain the "mystery of many tongues on which translation hinges" (Steiner 1975:57). The story has many versions, most of which tell about Pandora, the first woman of the Greek creation myth, releasing linguistic chaos as well as many other 'evils' from a lidded container (a box, a flask, an amphora) out of sheer curiosity. In these versions, it is an example of a myth that both stems from and supports misogynist notions about women.

*patriarchal language*: the language that is traditionally taught and used. Established, refined and regulated in largely male-run institutions such as universities, publishing houses, dictionaries, grammar and reference books, it reflects and maintains the values of these institutions. Because of the traditional male-bias of these institutions, it excludes or denigrates references to women and women's activities, interests, experiences. Feminist critique of patriarchal language includes criticism of clichéd dictionary entries, conventional grammar, proverbs and metaphors, job designations, and language use in all public domains.

*phallocentric order*, also *phallologocentric*: a neologism used in feminist and deconstructionist theories to express the authority assigned to and wielded by the 'Phallus' in Freudian/Lacanian thought and assumed by men in patriarchy; 'phallologocentric' carries the additional meaning of 'logos' (word) and expresses the control of language in patriarchy.

*'political correctness' reaction*: the reaction by largely conservative forces against the attempts made in North America over the past thirty years to produce and use inclusive language, i.e. language that acknowledges women and other 'marginal' groups and refrains from imposing 'white male middle-class' norms on a multi-ethnic and pluralistic society.

*polysemous/polysemic*: terms describing the fact that language is ambiguous and that many words can have more than one meaning. Polysemous terms have been used creatively by feminist (and other) writers to undermine conventional notions about language, and particularly 'patriarchal language', expressing a single and clear meaning that everyone agrees upon.

*radical feminism*: the form of feminism that seeks to get at the root causes of misogyny, arguing that they are located in issues of sexuality. It thus focuses its critical analyses and creative writing on sexual relations and pays attention to personal rather than public lives of women.

*sexism*: discrimination on the basis of biological sex; usually refers to the discrimination against women.

*socialization*: the processes through which humans learn how to behave and live in society.

*women's movement*: the broad grassroots movement that developed in the 1960s in most western countries and which incorporates various types of feminist thought and activism. It includes all those women who support feminist ideals and projects but do not necessarily take radical political stands themselves.

# Bibliographical References

*For easy reference, the texts dealing specifically with issues of gender and translation are marked with an asterisk. Brief annotations have been included where appropriate.*

Alarcón, Norma (1983) 'Chicana's Feminist Literature: A Re-Vision Through Malintzin/ or Malintzin: Putting Flesh Back on the Object', in Cherríe Moraga and Gloria Anzaldúa (eds) *This Bridge Called My Back. Writings by Radical Women of Color*, New York: Kitchen Table, Women of Color Press, 182-90.

Alarcón, Norma (1989) 'Traddutora, Traditora: A Paradigmatic Figure of Chicana Feminism', *Cultural Critique*, Fall Issue: 57-87.

Alcoff, Linda (1994) 'Cultural Feminism versus Post-Structuralism: The Identity Crisis in Feminist Theory', in Nicholas B. Dirks, Geoff Eley and Sherry B. Ortner (eds) *A Reader in Contemporary Social Theory*, Princeton, N.J.: Princeton University Press, 96-122.

*An Inclusive Language Lectionary* (1983) Philadelphia: Westminster Press.

Ankum, Katharina von (1993) 'The Difficulty of Saying 'I': Translation and Censorship of Christa Wolf's *Der geteilte Himmel*', *Studies in 20th Century Literature* 17(2): 223-41.

*Arrojo, Rosemary (1994) 'Fidelity and the Gendered Translation', *TTR* 7(2): 147-64.

*Arrojo, Rosemary (1995) 'Feminist 'Orgasmic' Theories of Translation and their Contradictions', *TradTerm* 2: 67-75. *A critical response to Susan Bassnett's 1992 text on questions of gender and translation.*

Banting, Pamela (1992) 'Body Inc.: Daphne Marlatt's Translation Poetics', in Janice Williamson (ed) *Holic/Hilac. Women's Writing and the Literary Tradition*, Edmonton, Alberta: Research Institute for Comparative Literature, University of Alberta, 1-19.

Barnard, Mary (1958) *Sappho. A New Translation* (Foreword by Dudley Fitts), Berkeley, CA: University of California Press.

Barthes, Roland (1973) *Le plaisir du texte*, Paris: Editions du Seuil.

*Bassnett, Susan (1992) 'Writing in No Man's Land: Questions of Gender and Translation', *Ilha Do Desterro, Studies in Translation* 28: 63-73. *Bassnett links gender issues with burgeoning translation studies in the late seventies.*

Batchelor, Jane (1995) 'Changing the Agenda: Gender Consciousness in Relation to Louise Labé's Sonnets'. Paper presented at the EST Congress in Prague, September 1995.

Beauvoir, Simone de (1949) *Le Deuxième Sexe*, Paris: Gallimard, trans. by Howard Parshley as *The Second Sex*, New York: Knopf, 1952.

Beauvoir, Simone de (1954) *Les Mandarins*, Paris: Gallimard, trans. by Leonard Friedman as *The Mandarins*, Cleveland: World Publishing, 1956.

Berman, Antoine (1995) *Pour une critique de la traduction: John Donne*, Paris: Gallimard.

Bersianik, Louky (1976) *L'Euguelionne*, Montreal: Stanké, trans. by Howard Scott as *L'Eugelion*, Montreal: Alter Ego Press, 1997.

Bonner, Maria (1985) 'Norwegalitanisch und deutegalitanisch: Zur Sprache in *Egalias dotre* und *Die Töchter Egalias*', in Heinrich Beck (ed) *Arbeiten zur Skandinavistik*, Frankfurt: Peter Lang.

Boucher, Denise (1979) *Les fées ont soif*, Montreal: Éditions Intermède, trans. by Alan Brown as *The Fairies are Thirsty*, Vancouver: Talonbooks, 1982.

Bourjea, Michelle (1986) 'Agua Viva, au fils des mots. Analyse critique de la traduction en français de *Agua Viva* de Clarice Lispector', *Meta* 31(3): 258-71.

*Bratcher, R. G. (1991) 'Male-Oriented Language Originated by Bible Translators', in H. M. Orlinsky and R. G. Bratcher (eds) *A History of Bible Translation and the North American Contribution*, Atlanta: Scholars Press.

Brod, Harry (ed) (1987) *The Making of Masculinities: The New Men's Studies*, Boston: Allen and Unwin.

Brossard, Nicole (1977) *L'Amèr ou le chapitre effrité*, Montreal: Quinze.

Brossard, Nicole (1980) *Amantes*, Montreal: Quinze, trans. by Barbara Godard as *Lovhers*, Montreal: Guernica Editions, 1986.

Brossard, Nicole (1985) *La lettre aérienne*, Montreal: Les éditions du remue-ménage, trans. by Marlene Wildeman as *The Aerial Letter*, Toronto: The Women's Press, 1988.

Brossard, Nicole (1987) *Sous la Langue*, trans. by Susanne de Lotbinière-Harwood as *Under Tongue*, Montreal, L'Essentielle (bilingual edition).

Butler, Judith (1990) *Gender Trouble. Feminism and the Subversion of Identity*, London & New York: Routledge.

Cameron, Deborah (1985) *Feminism and Linguistic Theory*, Houndsmill, Basingstoke: The Macmillan Press.

Carson, Anne (1986) *Eros the Bittersweet*, Princeton, N.J.: Princeton University Press.

*Chamberlain, Lori (1988/1992) 'Gender and the Metaphorics of Translation', *Signs* 13: 454-72; reprinted in Lawrence Venuti (ed) *Rethinking Translation. Discourse, Subjectivity, Ideology*, London & New York: Routledge, 1992, 57-74. *An elaboration of the patriarchal metaphors in which discussion about translation has traditionally been formulated.*

Cixous, Hélène (1975) 'Le rire de la Méduse', *L'Arc* 61: 39-54, trans. by Keith Cohen and Paula Cohen as 'The Laugh of the Medusa', *Signs: Journal of Women in Culture and Society* 1(4): 875-93, 1976.

# Bibliography

Cixous, Hélène, Madeleine Gagnon and Annie Leclerc (1977) *La Venue à l'écriture*, Paris: Union générale d'édition.

Collins, Gina Michelle (1984) 'Translating a Feminine Discourse: Clarice Lispector's *Agua Viva*', in Marilyn Gaddis Rose (ed) *Translation Perspectives. Selected Papers 1982-1983*, Binghamton: SUNY Binghamton, 119-124.

Cordero, Anne D. (1990) 'Simone de Beauvoir Twice Removed', *Simone de Beauvoir Studies* 7: 49-56.

Cypess, Sandra Messinger (1991) *La Malinche in Mexican Literature: From History to Myth*, Austin: University of Texas Press.

Daly, Mary (1978) *Gyn/Ecology. The Metaethics of Radical Feminism*, Boston: Beacon Press, trans. by Erika Wisselinck as *Gyn/Ökologie, eine Meta-Ethik des radikalen Feminismus*, München: Frauenoffensive, 1980.

Daly, Mary and Jane Caputi (1987) *Websters' First New Intergalactic Wickedary of the English Language*, Boston: Beacon Press.

Damjanova, Ludmila (1993) 'Umgang mit Weiblichkeit in Sprichwörtern und in Alltagssprache (anhand von Beispielen aus dem Spanischen, Russischen, Bulgarischen und Deutschen)', paper presented at the Münchner Linguistik Tage, March 1993.

Davidson, Cathy N. (1994) 'Loose Change: Issues and Controversies in Women's Studies and American Studies', in G. Blaicher and B. Glaser (eds) *Anglistentag: Proceedings*, Tübingen: Niemeyer, 158-68.

DeJulio, Maryann (1994) 'On Translating Olympe de Gouges', in Doris Kadish and Françoise Massardier-Kenney (eds) *Translating Slavery: Gender and Race in French Women's Writing, 1783-1823*, Kent, Ohio: Kent State University Press, 125-34.

Del Castillo, Adelaida R. (1977) 'Malintzin Tenépal: A Preliminary Look into a New Perspective', in Rosaura Sánchez and Rosa Martinez Cruz (eds) *Essays on la Mujer*, Los Angeles: UCLA, Chicano Studies Centre, 124-49.

*Delisle, Jean (1993) 'Traducteurs médiévaux, traductrices féministes: une même éthique de la traduction?', *TTR* 6(1): 203-230.

Derrida, Jacques (1985) 'Des Tours de Babel', in Joseph F. Graham (ed) *Difference in Translation*, Ithaca, N.Y.: Cornell University Press, 165-248.

*Diaz-Diocaretz, Miriam (1985) *Translating Poetic Discourse: Questions on Feminist Strategies in Adrienne Rich*, Amsterdam & Philadelphia: John Benjamins.

Duras, Marguerite (1980) 'An Interview', in Elaine Marks and Irene de Courtivron (eds) *New French Feminisms*, trans. by Susan Husserl-Kapit, Amherst: University of Massachusetts Press, 174-76.

Eisenstein, Hester (1983) 'Introduction', in H. Eisenstein and A. Jardine (eds) *The Future of Difference*, New Brunswick, N.J.: Rutgers University Press, xv-xxiv.

*Ellingworth, P. (1987) 'Translating the Bible Inclusively', *Meta* 32(1): 46-54.

*Ellingworth, P. (1992) 'The Scope of Inclusive Language', *The Bible Translator* 43: 130-40.

Felski, Rita (1989) *Beyond Feminist Aesthetics. Feminist Literature and Social Change*, Cambridge, Mass.: Harvard University Press.

Fisken, Beth Wynne (1985) 'Mary Sidney's *Psalmes*: Education and Wisdom', in Margaret Patterson Hannay (ed) *Silent but for the Word. Tudor Women as Patrons, Translators, and Writers of Religious Works,* Ohio: The Kent State University Press, 166-83.

*Flotow, Luise von (1991) 'Feminist Translation: Contexts, Practices, Theories', *TTR* 4(2): 69-84.

*Flotow, Luise von (1994) 'Québec's 'Écriture au féminin' and Translation Politicized', in F. Eguiloz, R. Merino et al. (eds) *Transvases Culturales: Literatura, Cine, Traduccion*, Vitoria, Spain: Facultad de Filologia, Universida del Pais Vasco, 219-29.

Flotow, Luise von (1995) 'Translating Women of the Eighties: Eroticism, Anger, Ethnicity', in Sherry Simon (ed) *Culture in Transit: Translating the Literature of Quebec*, Montreal: Véhicule Press, 31-46.

*Flotow, Luise von (1996a) 'Weiblichkeit, Zweisprachigkeit und Übersetzung: Kanada', in Johan Strutz and Peter Zima (eds) *Literarische Polyphonie*, Tübingen: Günter Narr, 123-36.

*Flotow, Luise von (1996b) 'Legacies of *écriture au féminin*: Bilingual Transformances, Translation Politicized, Subaltern Versions of the Text of the Street', *Journal of Canadian Studies*, Spring Issue: 88-109.

*Flotow, Luise von (in press) 'Mutual Pun-ishment? The Translation of Feminist Wordplay: Mary Daly's *Gyn/Ecology* in German', in Dirk Delabastita (ed) *Traductio: Essays on Punning and Translation*, Manchester: St. Jerome Publishing & Namur: Presses Universitaires de Namur.

*Freiwald, Bina (1991) 'The Problem of Trans-Lation: Reading French Feminism', *TTR* 4(2): 55-68.

Funk, Nanette and Magda Mueller (eds) (1993) *Gender Politics and Post-Communism*, London & New York: Routledge.

Gaboriau, Linda (trans.) (1979)*A Clash of Symbols*, Toronto: The Coach House Press; translation of *La nef des sorcières* by Marthe Blackburn, Nicole Brossard et al, Montreal: Quinze, 1976.

*Gillam, Robyn (1995) 'The Mauve File Folder: Notes on the Translation of Nicole Brossard', *Paragraph* 16: 8-12.

Gilligan, Carol (1982) *In a Different Voice: Psychological Theory and Women's Development*, Cambridge, Mass.: Harvard University Press.

Gillman, Richard (1988) 'The Man Behind the Feminist Bible', *The New York Times Book Review*, May 22.

# Bibliography

*Godard, Barbara (1983) 'Translator's Preface', *These Our Mothers*, Toronto: Coach House Press; translation of Brossard (1977).

*Godard, Barbara (1984) 'Translating and Sexual Difference', *Resources for Feminist Research* 13(3): 13-16.

*Godard, Barbara (1986) 'Translator's Preface', *Lovhers*, Montreal: Guernica Editions; translation of Brossard (1980).

*Godard, Barbara (1990) 'Theorizing Feminist Discourse/Translation', in Susan Bassnett and André Lefevere (eds) *Translation, History, Culture*, London: Pinter Publishers. *This article establishes a link between women's double language and the doubling of languages that occurs in translation.*

*Godard, Barbara (1991a) 'Translator's Preface', *Picture Theory*, Montreal: Guernica Editions; translation of Nicole Brossard's *Picture Theory*, Montreal: Éditions Nouvelle Optique, 1982 (revised edition Montreal: L'Hexagone, 1989).

*Godard, Barbara (1991b) 'Translating Translating Translation', preface to *The Tangible Word*, an anthology of work by France Théoret, Montreal: Guernica Editions.

*Godard, Barbara (1991c) 'Translating (With) the Speculum', *TTR* 4(2): 85-121.

*Godard, Barbara (1995) 'Negotiating Relations', *Paragraph* 17: 39-40.

Goga, S. (1993) *Emanzipation und weibliches Selbstverständnis In Charlotte Brontes "Jane Eyre" und ausgewählten deutschen Übersetzungen*, masch. MA Thesis: University of Düsseldorf.

Goldberger, Avriel H. (1990) 'Germaine de Staël's *Corinne*: Challenges to the Translator in the 1980s', *The French Review* 63(5): 800-809.

Goldberger, Avriel H. (1994) 'Madame de Staël, *De l'esprit des traductions*: réflexions d'une traductrice', *Le Groupe de Coppet et l'Europe 1789-1830, Actes du 5ᵉ Colloque de Coppet*, Tübingen 8-10 juillet 1993, Lausanne: Institut Benjamin Constant & Paris: J. Touzot.

*Gooze, Marjanne E. (1995) 'A Language of Her Own: Bettina Brentano-von Arnim's Translation Theory and Her English Translation Project', in Elke Frederiksen and Katerine R. Goodman (eds) *Bettina Brentano-von Arnim: Gender and Politics*, Detroit: Wayne State University Press, 278-303.

Hamm, Maggie (1987) 'Translation as Survival: Zora Neale Hurston and La Malincha', *Fiction International* 17(2): 120-29.

*Hannay, Margaret Patterson (ed) (1985) *Silent But for the Word: Tudor Women as Patrons, Translators, and Writers of Religious Works*, Kent: Kent State University Press. *An anthology that examines women's roles and the issue of gender in the field of publishing, writing and translating in Tudor England.*

Harel, Michal (1993) *La Transposition de l'"Ecriture féminine" du français à l'hébreu*, Mémoire de maîtrise, Tel Aviv: University of Tel Aviv.

*Haugerud, Joann (1977) *The Word for Us, Gospels of John and Mark, Epistles to the Romans and the Galatians*, Seattle: Coalition of Women in Religion. *An important work on gender issues in Bible translation.*

Hoefkens, Ivo R.V. (1994) 'Marguerite Yourcenar, traductrice', *Babel* 40(1): 21-37.

Irigaray, Luce (1977) *Ce sexe qui n'en est pas un*, Paris: Les éditions de minuit.

Johnson, Barbara (1985) 'Taking Fidelity Philosophically', in Joseph F. Graham (ed) *Difference in Translation,* Ithaca & London: Cornell University Press, 142-47.

*Jouve, Nicole Ward (1991) *White Woman Speaks With Forked Tongue: Criticism as Autobiography*, London: Routledge.

*Kadish, Doris and Françoise Massardier-Kenney (eds) (1994) *Translating Slavery: Gender and Race in French Women's Writing, 1783-1823*, Kent: Kent State University Press. *A collection of French source texts and their English translations accompanied by essays that discuss issues of gender, race and feminist politics in the practice of translation.*

Kamuf, Peggy (ed) (1991) *A Derrida Reader. Between the Blinds*, Hemel Hempstead: Harvester Wheatsheaf.

Kaplan, Cora (1976) 'Language and Gender', *Essays on Culture and Feminism*, London: Verso, 69-93.

Kaufman, Michael (ed) (1987) *Beyond Patriarchy: Essays by Men on Pleasure, Power and Change*, New York: Oxford University Press.

Keefe, Terry (1994) 'Another Silencing of Beauvoir. Guess what's missing this time?', *French Studies* 50 (Spring Supplement): 18-29.

Klaw, Barbara (1995) 'Sexuality in Beauvoir's *Les mandarins*', in Margaret A. Simons (ed) *Feminist Interpretations of Simone de Beauvoir*, University Park, Pennsylvania: The Pennsylvania State University Press, 193-222.

Koerner, Charlotte (1984) 'Divided Heaven — A Sacrifice of Message and Meaning in Translation', *Germanic Quarterly* 57(4): 213-30.

Kolias, Helen Denidrou (trans.) (1989) *My Story* (translation of 1881 original by Elizavet Moutzan-Martinengou), Athens: University of Georgia Press.

*Kolias, Helen Denidrou (1990) 'Empowering the Minor: Translating Women's Autobiography', *Journal of Modern Greek Studies* 8: 213-21.

*Krontiris, Tina (1992) *Oppositional Voices: Women as Writers and Translators of Literature in the English Renaissance*, London & New York: Routledge.

Lamb, Mary Ellen (1985) 'The Cooke Sisters: Attitudes toward Learned Women in the Renaissance', in Margaret Patterson Hannay (ed) *Silent but for the Word. Tudor Women as Patrons, Translators and Writers of Religious Works*, Kent, Ohio: The Kent State University Press, 107-125.

Lattimore, Richard (ed/trans) (1949/1960) *Greek Lyrics*, Chicago: University of Chicago Press.)

Lefevere, André (1992) *Translation, Rewriting and the Manipulation of Literary Fame*, London & New York: Routledge.

*Levine, Suzanne Jill (1983/1992) 'Translation as (Sub)Version : On Translating *Infante's Inferno*', *SubStance* 42: 85-94. Reprinted in Lawrence Venuti (ed) *Rethinking Translation. Discourse, Subjectivity, Ideology*, London & New York: Routledge, 75-85. *One of the first texts to position the contemporary woman translator in the role of possible parodist of 'offensive' discourse.*

*Levine, Suzanne Jill (1991) *The Subversive Scribe: Translating Latin American Fiction*, Minneapolis, Minn.: Greywolf Press.

Lewis, Reina (1996) *Gendering Orientalism*, London & New York: Routledge.

*Littau, Karin (1995a) 'Refractions of the Feminine: The Monstrous Transformations of Lulu', *Modern Language Notes* 110(4): 888-912.

Littau, Karin (1995b) 'Pandora's Tongues', paper presented at the EST Congress in Prague, September 1995.

Lobb, Frances (ed/trans) (1950) *The Twenty-Four Sonnets: Louise Labé, La Belle Cordière*, London: Euphorion Press.

Lorde, Audre (1981) 'The Master's Tools Will Never Dismantle The Master's House'. in Cherrie Moraga and Gloria Anzaldúa (eds) *This Bridge Called My Back. Writings by Radical Women of Color*, New York, Kitchen Table: Women of Color Press.

*Lotbinière-Harwood, Suzanne de (1986) 'Translating Nicole Brossard', *Writing Magazine* 16: 36-41.

*Lotbinière-Harwood, Suzanne de (1989) 'About the *her* in other', Preface to *Letters from an Other* by Lise Gauvin, Toronto: The Women's Press.

*Lotbinière-Harwood, Suzanne de (1991) *Re-Belle et Infidèle. La Traduction comme pratique de réécriture au féminin/The Body Bilingual. Translation as a Rewriting in the Feminine*, Toronto: The Women's Press & Montreal: les éditions du remue-ménage. *A comprehensive, praxis-based descriptive accounting of the many ways in which gender issues impinge upon translation.*

*Lotbinière-Harwood, Suzanne de (1994) 'Acting the (Re)Writer: a feminist translator's practice of space', *Fireweed* 44/45: 101-110.

Lotbinière-Harwood, Suzanne de (1995) 'Geo-graphies of Why', in Sherry Simon (ed) *Culture in Transit*, Montreal: Véhicule Press.

*Maier, Carol (1985) 'A Woman in Translation, Reflecting', *Translation Review* 17: 4-8.

*Maier, Carol (1992) 'Women in Translation: Current Intersections, Theory, Practice', *Delos* 5(2): 29-39.

*Maier, Carol and Françoise Massardier-Kenney (1996) 'Gender in/and Literary Translation', in Marilyn Gaddis Rose (ed) *Translation Horizons. Beyond the Boundaries of 'Translation Spectrum'* (Translation Perspectives IX), Binghamton: SUNY Binghamton, Center for Research in Translation, 225-42.

Marks, Elaine and Isabelle de Courtivron (eds) (1980) *New French Feminisms. An Anthology*, Amherst: The University of Massachusetts Press.

*Marlatt, Daphne (1989) 'Translating Mauve: Reading Writing', *Tessera* 6: 27-30.

Massardier-Kenney, Françoise (1994) 'Translation Theory and Practice', in Doris Kadish and Françoise Massardier-Kenney (eds) *Translating Slavery: Gender and Race in French Women's Writing, 1783-1823*, Kent, Ohio: Kent State University Press, 11-25.

McClintock, Anne (1995) *Imperial Leather: Race, Gender and Sexuality in the Colonial Contest*, London & New York: Routledge.

*Meurer, S. (ed) (1993) *Die vergessenen Schwestern. Frauengerechte Sprache in der Bibelübersetzung*, Stuttgart: Deutsche Bibelgesellschaft.

*Mezei, Kathy (1986) 'The Question of Gender in Translation: Examples from Denise Boucher and Anne Hébert: A Corollary to Evelyne Voldeng's 'Trans/lata/ latus'', *Canadian Fiction Magazine* 57: 136-41.

Miller, Barbara Stoler, Nabaneeta Dev Sen and Agueda Pizarro de Rayo (1978) 'Splitting the Mother Tongue: Bengali and Spanish Poems in English Translations', *Signs* 3(3): 608-621.

Miller, Casey and Kate Swift (1976) *Words and Women: New Language in New Times*, Garden City, NY: Anchor Press.

Mirandé, Alfredo and Evangelina Enríquez (1979) *La Chicana. The Mexican-American Woman*, Chicago & London: The University of Chicago Press.

Mohanty, Chandra T. (1984) 'Under Western Eyes: Feminist Scholarship and Colonial Discourses', *Boundary 2* 12(3) and 13(1): 333-58.

Moraga, Cherrie and Gloria Anzaldúa (eds) (1983) *This Bridge is Called My Back: Writings by Radical Women of Color*, New York: Kitchen Table, Women of Color Press.

Morgan, Robin (1968) *Going Too Far. The Personal Chronicle of a Feminist*, New York: Random House.

Newmark, Peter (1991) *About Translation*, Clevedon: Multilingual Matters.

Nida, Eugene (1995) 'Names and Titles', unpublished manuscript.

Niedzwiecki, Patricia (1993) 'Women and Language', *Cahier des Femmes d'Europe* 40: 1-31.

*Nölle-Fischer, Karen (1995) 'Können weibliche Schreibweisen Bewegung in die Geschlechterbeziehungen bringen?', *Der Übersetzer* 29(1): 1-8.

O'Connell, Eithne (1995) 'Twice Marginalized: The Translation of Contemporary Irish Women's Poetry', paper presented at the EST Congress in

Prague, September 1995.

O'Leary, Veronique and Louise Toupin (eds) (1982) *Québécoises deboutte*, 2 volumes, Montreal: les éditions du remue-ménage.

Orlinsky, H. M. and R. G. Bratcher (eds) (1991) *A History of Bible Translation and the North American Contribution*, Atlanta: Scholars Press.

Panofsky, Dora and Erwin Panofsky (1962) *Pandora's Box: The Changing Aspects of a Mythical Symbol,* New York: Pantheon Book.

*Parker, Alice (1993) 'Under the Covers: A Synaesthesia of Desire (Lesbian Translations)', in Susan J. Wolfe and Julia Penelope (eds) *Sexual Practice, Textual Theory: Lesbian Cultural Criticism*, Cambridge & Oxford: Blackwell, 322-39.

Patterson, Yolande (1992) 'Who was this H.M. Parshley?: The Saga of Translating Simone de Beauvoir's *The Second Sex*', *Simone de Beauvoir Studies* 9: 41-47.

*Penrod, Lynn K. (1993) 'Translating Hélène Cixous: French Feminism(s) and Anglo-American Feminist Theory', *TTR* 6(2): 39-54.

Peretz, Maya (1992) 'A Female Poet and her Male Translator: A Case Study', *Trabalhos en Linguistica Aplicada* 19: 41-47.

*Porter, Catherine (1987) 'Translating French Feminism: Luce Irigaray's *Ce Sexe qui n'en est pas un*', in Marilyn Gaddis Rose (ed) *Translation Perspectives III. Selected Papers, 1985-86*, Binghamton: SUNY Binghamton, 40-52.

Prescott, Anne Lake (1985) 'The Pearl of the Valois and Elizabeth I: Marguerite de Navarre's *Miroir* and Tudor England', in Margaret Patterson Hannay (ed) *Silent but for the Word. Tudor Women as Patrons, Translators, and Writers of Religious Works*, Kent, Ohio: The Kent State University Press, 61-76.

*Prins, Yopie (in press) 'Sappho's Afterlife in Translation', in E. Greene (ed) *Rereading Sappho: Reception and Transmission*, Berkeley: University of California Press.

Prokosch, Frederick (ed/trans) (1947) *Love Sonnets by Louise Labé*, New York: New Directions.

Prudhoe, John (trans.) (1979) *Torquato Tasso*, Manchester: Manchester University Press.

*Pusch, Luise (1984) 'Eine männliche Seefrau! Der blödeste Ausdruck seit Wibschengedenken. Über Gerd Brantenbergs *Die Töchter Egalias*', in *Das Deutsche als Männersprache*, Frankfurt: Suhrkamp, 69-75.

*Pusch, Luise (1990) 'Mary, please don't pun-ish us any more! Mary Daly, die Sprach und die deutschsprachige Leserin', in *Alle Menschen werden Schwestern*, Frankfurt: Suhrkamp, 104-111.

Raschkow, I. N. (1990) *Upon the Dark Places. Anti-Semitism and Sexism in English Renaissance Biblical Translation*, Sheffield: Academic Press.

Rayor, Diane (1991) *Sappho's Lyre. Archaic Lyric and Women Poets of Ancient Greece*, Berkeley: University of California Press.

Rayor, Diane (1992) 'Translating Sappho: Who Speaks?', unpublished paper, MLA conference.

*Reiß, Katharina (1993) 'Frauengerechte Sprache?', in S. Meurer (ed) *Die vergessenen Schwestern: Frauengerechte Sprache in der Bibelübersetzung*, Stuttgart: Deutsche Bibelgesellschaft, 37-52.

*Robinson, Douglas (1995) 'Theorizing Translation in a Woman's Voice: Subverting the Rhetoric of Patronage, Courtly Love and Morality', *The Translator* 1(2): 153-75.

Rosaldo, Michelle (1980) 'The Use and Abuse of Anthropology: Reflections on Feminist and Cross-Cultural Understanding', *Signs: Journal of Women in Culture and Society* 5(3): 389-417.

Schmitt, J. J. (1992) 'God's Wife: Some Gender Reflections on the Bible and Biblical Interpretation', in L. A. M. Perry, L. H. Turner and H. M. Sterk (eds) *Constructing and Reconstructing Gender: The Links Among Communication, Language and Gender*, New York: State University of New York Press, 269-81.

Schreck, N. and M. Leech (1986) *Psalms Anew. In Inclusive Language*, Winona, MN: Saint Mary's Press.

Scott, Gail (1989) 'Red Tin + White Tulle. On Memory and Writing', in *Spaces Like Stairs*, Toronto: The Women's Press, 15-27.

Scott, Howard (1984) 'Louky Bersianik's *L'Euguelionne*: Problems of Translating the Critique of Language in New Quebec Feminist Writing'. Unpublished Master's thesis, Montreal: Concordia University.

*Scott, Howard (1989) 'Translator's Introduction', *Lair*, Toronto: Coach House Press; translation of *Antre* by Madeleine Gagnon, Montreal: Editions du remue-ménage.

Scott, Nina M. (1988) "If you are not pleased to favor me, put me out of your mind ...' Gender and Authority in Sor Juana Inés de la Cruz: And the Translation of Her Letter to the Reverend Father Maestro Antonio Nunez of the Society of Jesus', *Women's Studies International Forum* 11(5): 429-38.

Showalter, Elaine (ed) (1986) *The New Feminist Criticism. Essays on Women, Literature and Theory*, London: Virago Press.

*Simon, Sherry (ed) (1995) *Culture in Transit. Translating the Literature of Quebec*, Montreal: Vehicule Press.

*Simon, Sherry (1996) *Gender and Translation. Culture and Identity and the Politics of Transmission,* London & New York: Routledge. *First comprehensive study of gender issues in numerous types of translation, largely focused on the Anglo-American situation.*

*Simons, Margaret (1983) 'The Silencing of Simone de Beauvoir: Guess What's Missing from *The Second Sex*', *Women's Studies International*

*Forum* 6(5): 559-64.

Simons, Margaret (ed) (1995) *Feminist Interpretations of Simone de Beauvoir*, University Park, Pennsylvania: The Pennsylvania State University Press.

Sirois, Andrée (1997) *Les femmes dans l'histoire de la traduction: domaine français de la Renaissance au 20e siècle*, MA Thesis, Ottawa: University of Ottawa.

Spender, Dale (1980) *Man Made Language*, New York & London: Routledge & Kegan Paul.

*Spivak, Gayatri Chakavorty (1988) *In Other Worlds: Essays in Cultural Politics*, New York & London: Routledge.

*Spivak, Gayatri Chakavorty (1992) 'The Politics of Translation', in Michèle Barrett and Anne Phillips (eds) *Destabilizing Theory*, Stanford, CA: Stanford University Press.

*Stark, Suzanne (1993) 'Women and Translation in the Nineteenth Century', *New Comparison* 15: 33-44.

Stefan, Verena (1975) *Häutungen*, München: Frauenoffensive, trans. by Johanna Moore and Beth Weckmueller as *Shedding*, New York: Daughters Publishing, 1978; reprinted in Verena Stefan *Shedding and Literally Dreaming*, New York: The Feminist Press at the City University of New York, 1994.

Steiner, George (1975) *After Babel. Aspects of Language and Translation*, Oxford: Oxford University Press.

Tharu, Susie and K. Lalita (eds) (1991/1993) *Women Writing in India*, Vols. 1 and 2, New York: The Feminist Press at the City University of New York.

Thill, Beate (1995) 'Translation and Female Identity', paper presented at the EST Congress in Prague, September 1995.

Thorne, Barrie, Cheris Kramarae and Nancy Henley (eds) (1983) *Language, Gender and Society*, Rowley, Mass.: Newbury House.

Tolbert, M. (1990) *Language about God in Liturgy and Scripture. A Study Guide*, Philadelphia: Fortress Press.

*Tostevin, Lola Lemire (1989) 'Contamination: A Relation of Differences', *Tessera* 6: 13-14.

Trible, Ph. (1973) 'Depatriarchalizing in Biblical Interpretation', *Journal of the American Academy of Religion* 41: 30-48.

Trible, Ph. (1978) *God and the Rhetoric of Sexuality. Overtures to Biblical Theology*, Philadelphia: Fortress Press.

Tröml-Plötz, Senta (1982) *Frauensprache: Sprache der Veränderung*, Frankfurt: Fischer.

Vanderauwera, Ria (1985) *Dutch Novels Translated Into English. The Transformation of a 'Minority' Literature*, Amsterdam: Rodopi.

Venuti, Lawrence (ed) (1992) *Rethinking Translation. Discourse, Subjectivity, Ideology*, London & New York: Routledge.

Verbrugge, Rita (1985) 'Margaret More Roper's Personal Expression in the *Devout Treatise Upon the Pater Noster*', in Margaret Patterson Hannay (ed) *Silent but for the Word. Tudor Women as Patrons, Translators, and Writers of Religious Works*, Kent, Ohio: The Kent State University Press, 30-42.

*Voldeng, Evelyne (1984) 'Translata/Translatus', *Room of One's Own* 8(4): 82-96.

*Voldeng, Evelyne (1985) 'The Elusive Source Text' (Review of *These Our Mothers* by Nicole Brossard, trans. by Barbara Godard), *Canadian Literature* 105: 138-39.

Vries, Anneke de (1996) 'Scheef licht: Gender-stereotypen in vertalingen van Richteren 4', *Filter, Tijdschrift voor vertalenen vertaalwetenschap* 3(1): 44-53. [False Light: Gender stereotypes in (Dutch) translations of Judges 4]

Vries, Anneke de (1997a) 'Meisje, duifje, zusje, schaapje. Gender-stereotypen in vertalingen van Hooglied', *Tijdschrift voor Vrouwenstudies* 69(1): 49-60. [Little girl, little dove, little sister, little sheep. Gender stereotypes in (Dutch) translations of the Song of Songs]

Vries Anneke de (1997b) 'A Matter of Life and Death: Gender Stereotypes in Some Modern Dutch Biblical Translation', in *Translation as Intercultural Communication. Selected Papers from the EST Congress, Prague 1995*, Amsterdam & Philadelphia: John Benjamins.

*Wildemann, Marlene (1989) 'Daring Deeds: Translation as Lesbian Feminist Language Act', *Tessera: La traduction au féminin, Translating Women* 6: 31-41.

Wilson, Katharina (ed) (1988) *Women Writers of the Renaissance and Reformation*, Athens, GA: University of Georgia Press.

Wittig, Monique and Sande Zeig (1981) *Borrador para un dictionario de las amantes: Draft of a Dictionary for Lovers*, New York: French and European Publications.

Wolf, Christa (1963) *Der Geteilte Himmel*, Halle: Mitteldeutscher Verlag, trans. by Joan Becker as *Divided Heaven*, East Berlin: Seven Seas Verlag, 1965. Translation reprinted New York: Adler's Foreign Books, 1981.

*Zwarg, Christina (1990) 'Feminism in Translation: Margaret Fuller's Tasso', *Studies in Romanticism* 29: 463-90.

## Special Issues of Journals

*Tessera* (1989) 'La Traduction au féminin/Translating Women'.

*Yale French Studies* (1981) 'Feminist Readings: French Texts/American Contexts'.

TRANSLATION THEORIES EXPLAINED
Series Editor: Anthony Pym, Spain
ISSN 1365-0513

## Other Titles in the Series

*Translating as a Purposeful Activity*, Christiane Nord
*Translation and Gender*, Luise von Flotow
*Translation and Language*, Peter Fawcett
*Translation and Empire*, Douglas Robinson
*Conference Interpreting*, Roderick Jones
*Translation and Literary Criticism*, Marilyn Gaddis Rose

### Forthcoming in 1998

*Contemporary Approaches to Translation Teaching*, Donald Kiraly
*Translation in Systems*, Theo Hermans

## Also Available from St. Jerome

*Dictionary of Translation Studies*, Mark Shuttleworth & Moira Cowie
*Western Translation Theory from Herodotus to Nietzsche*, Douglas
Robinson
*Wordplay and Translation*, edited by Dirk Delabastita
*Traductio. Essays on Punning and Translation*, edited by Dirk
Delabastita
*Method in Translation History*, Anthony Pym

### *Plus*

*The Translator. Studies in Intercultural Communication*, a refereed
international journal edited by Mona Baker

#0323 - 111016 - C0 - 234/156/7 - PB - 9781900650052